NOT I, NOT OTHER THAN I

For over half a century Russel Williams has been an utterly authentic voice of the Buddha dharma and spiritual friend to many. His goodness and wisdom shine through the pages of this book.

Lama Jampa Thaye, scholar, author, meditation master, founder of the Dechen International Association of Sakya and Karma Kagyu Tibetan Buddhist Centres

One of the most remarkable and powerful spiritual teachers of our time, who has been happy to remain almost unknown for several decades, sharing his wisdom and his presence to small groups of people, quietly changing many lives. With this book, Russel's profound teachings reach out to the wider world for the first time.

Steve Taylor, author of *The Fall, Waking From Sleep* and *The Calm Center*

There are a few who manage realisation easily, through some fluke, or perhaps through the work of past lives. We should draw near to them and listen carefully to what they have to say, to be inspired by their example, and for the constant reminder of the simplicity of our path. This eloquent book of Russel Williams' words of wisdom provides that inspiration beautifully.

Nick Scott, meditation teacher, co-author of *Rude Awakenings* and *The Long Road North*

May these words "from the heart" touch the hearts of those who read them and give them cc   he practice that leads to awakenir

Karuniko Bhikkhu, Chithurst

T0167563

Not I, Not Other Than I

The Life and Spiritual Teachings
of Russel Williams

Not I, Not Other Than I

The Life and Spiritual Teachings
of Russel Williams

Russel Williams
Edited by Steve Taylor

BOOKS

Winchester, UK
Washington, USA

First published by O-Books, 2015
O-Books is an imprint of John Hunt Publishing Ltd., Laurel House, Station Approach,
Alresford, Hants, SO24 9JH, UK
office1@jhpbooks.net
www.johnhuntpublishing.com

For distributor details and how to order please visit the 'Ordering' section on our website.

ISBN: 978 1 78279 729 6
Library of Congress Control Number: 2014954851

A CIP catalogue record for this book is available from the British Library.

Design: Stuart Davies

Printed and bound by CPI Group (UK) Ltd, Croydon, CR0 4YY, UK

We operate a distinctive and ethical publishing philosophy in all
areas of our business, from our global network of authors to
production and worldwide distribution.

CONTENTS

Introduction

by Steve Taylor

Russel Williams is a simple man. On the surface, you would think of him as a fairly typical man of his generation, although perhaps one who looks unusually young and sprightly for his 93 years. If you visited him at home with his wife Joyce, you wouldn't find anything unusual there either. Again, it would strike you as a fairly typical house for a couple of their senior years.

Russel is not educated – he left school at the age of 11 (in 1932) and has had no formal education since. He's not an intellectual; he hasn't read a great many books, and in his teachings he rarely refers to texts or other sources. Although he has been the president of the Buddhist Society of Manchester since 1974, and sometimes uses Buddhist terms or talks about the Buddha as an individual, he doesn't consider himself a Buddhist. He certainly doesn't 'teach' Buddhism in any formal sense.

As a result, Russel's spiritual teachings are very 'naked' and pure – that is, they are very free of theories, concepts and categories. This gives his teachings a rare clarity and power. There is no system. There are no rituals or rules to follow, no ideas to take on board. You don't have to believe anything. You don't have to accept anything. You don't have to become anything. All you have to do is be.

Russel often says that he's not interested in convincing people of anything. He encourages people to play with his teachings, to question them, to find out for themselves whether they are true. He doesn't think of himself as a guru, and has no desire to accumulate followers or disciples. Everything he teaches stems very directly from a particular state of being, one which he experiences as his constant reality, and which he has done for almost 65 years. There are many different terms for this state: stillness, pure consciousness, emptiness of being, the essence of our being, our true nature...

Russel teaches us how to uncover this state – how we can nurture it, and remove some of the obstacles which stop its expression. He makes it clear that this is our natural state, and that it's only due to confusion that we have lost access to it. He helps us to remove the confusion, to disentangle our minds from the mess of concepts and thinking habits which cloud them, so that we can become who we really are.

In this state, we are naturally one with everything, and with the universe itself. We are part of the Unmanifest. We are part of the pure consciousness which has given rise to the whole universe. That consciousness is our true nature, and when we rest within it, we feel a powerful sense of ease and contentment.

Since the late 1950s, Russel has held regular talks at the premises of the Buddhist Society of Manchester. Initially these were held almost every evening, but over the last few decades, they have taken place twice a week, on Monday and Wednesday evenings. Apart from missing the occasional week due to ill health, the meetings continue from year to year, unbroken. They are free of charge – on principle, Russel has never made any money from his spiritual teachings. The meetings are also completely open – anyone is free to come, and no one has ever been turned away.

Russel has never promoted or publicised himself. You won't find any of his talks advertised on the Internet or any videos of his on YouTube. Until now, he has never published any writings. He has always believed that he can be most effective working with small groups, helping to bring about change by intensively engaging with individuals.

I first suggested the idea of him writing a book several years ago. He was initially dismissive, saying that his teachings were most effective on a "feeling level", and that this could never be captured in writing. He was happy to let me interview him and tell his story in my book *Out of the Darkness*, but said he had no desire to publish a book of his own. For a long time, I encouraged him to record the twice-weekly meetings, so that they could be transcribed and perhaps eventually published, but again, he was not enthusiastic.

However, about three years ago I learned that Russel was now open to the idea of writing and publishing a book. Nearing the age of 90, he was aware that it might not be too long before he departed this Earth, and felt that it might be helpful to leave a record of his teachings. As a result, we began to record some of the meetings.

Knowing that Russel's early life was filled with many tragic and dramatic events, I was keen for the book to be partly an autobiography. Even from a purely historical point of view, his life story is fascinating: the terrible hardship of his life during the 1920s and 30s (particularly after being orphaned by the age of 11), his experiences at Dunkirk and during the Blitz, and his wanderings after the war. This leads to the story of his sudden spiritual awakening – one of the most amazing examples of 'transformation through suffering' I have come across.

We decided that an autobiography and a book of teachings would complement each other well, which led to the idea of setting them out as alternate chapters. As a result, I began to spend time with Russel at his home in Atherton (near Manchester), recording his recollections and memories of his life. I typed the recordings up, edited them, then handed the printed pages to him, for corrections and additions.

I spent two years working on the book on/off, but it never felt onerous. It was a labour of love, and a privilege, both to spend time with Russel and to delve so deeply into his teachings.

I first heard about Russel back in 1997. I had become friendly with a fellow spiritual seeker called Tony, whom I met at a Gurdjieff group. One evening, in his flat, I asked him, "Do you think you've ever met anyone who is enlightened?"

"Well, there's a man in Sale [a suburb of Manchester] who some people think is enlightened," he told me. "Very few people know about him, although he's been teaching for decades."

I accompanied Tony to one of Russel's meetings the following week. I was initially slightly sceptical. Russel didn't look like a spiritual teacher. He wore large black-rimmed glasses, had combed-back white hair and was formally dressed in a jacket and white shirt and tie. He was hard of hearing, and spoke very quietly, but clearly. I was aware of a few other English spiritual teachers of his generation, such as Alan Watts, Douglas Harding and Bede Griffiths. But Russel seemed different to them. He definitely wasn't from the upper echelons of the British class system. Although he had a fairly nondescript southern English accent, you could tell his background was humble and ordinary.

Like many people, I had quite an esoteric concept of spirituality and enlightenment. I associated those terms with Eastern traditions; they conjured up images of Indian gurus with long beards and long flowing robes, or monks with shaven heads. I had also been conditioned into thinking of enlightenment as a rare and unattainable state, something which only a few Indian or Tibetan adepts – and perhaps a few ascetic Christian mystics – had attained. So the idea that this ordinary looking 76 year old (as he was at that time) Englishman could be enlightened seemed a little bizarre.

However, Russel struck me immediately as an extremely wise person, who had found deep contentment and had a passionate desire to share it with others. I appreciated the purity and directness of his teachings straight away. I began to attend the meetings regularly, and after a while I noticed that after each visit, there was a powerful sense of well-being inside me – a feeling of lightness and calmness – which lasted for most of the next day and sometimes longer.

Nevertheless, it took me a few years to absorb the full power of Russel's teachings and of his being. This was probably because I initially took an intellectual approach to his teachings, analysing and interpreting them in the light of other spiritual traditions and teachings. But gradually I began to switch off to the intellectual aspect, and to shift into more of a 'feeling' mode. I didn't do this consciously; it was just a process which occurred naturally over the first years that I attended Russel's talks.

I began to experience very powerful altered states of consciousness during the meetings, which I still experience nowadays. These are quite difficult to describe, but they usually begin with a feeling of stillness, and a sense of energy slowing down and intensifying inside me. Then there is a sense of light, glowing brighter until it seems to engulf all objects in the room in a golden radiance. All objects seem to lose separateness, to merge into the radiance. I no longer feel any separateness; the notions of inside and outside lose significance. My inside is also outside, and vice versa. There is a tremendous sense of serenity. When I look around the room, there is a feeling of complete unfamiliarity, as if this is the first time I've ever been in it, and as if all the people and the objects around me are completely new to me…

At that point I'll give up trying to describe the state. For some reason, it seems to be most powerful – and to happen most easily – when Russel is talking to me and looking directly at me.

This is perhaps the most important aspect of Russel's teaching: the power of his being, and the feeling of oneness and deep serenity he generates through his being. Almost everybody who attends the meetings experiences this – although it might manifest itself in different ways – and it's probably the main reason why they keep coming back. (Some people have been regularly attending the meetings for 40 years or more. Even though I've been going for 17 years now, I still think of myself as a relative newcomer.)

Over the years, Russel's teachings and his being have had a

powerful cumulative effect on me. Looking back, I can sense that they have affected me in ways which I am only barely conscious of. They have seeped into my being and become a part of me. They have deepened, expanded and stabilised my spiritual experience. Thousands of people who have encountered Russel directly over the last few decades will vouch for the same. And hopefully many thousands more will have a similar experience through reading this book.

It's a great privilege to introduce the teachings of this almost unknown figure – one of the most remarkable and powerful spiritual teachers of our time, and possibly of all time – to a wider audience.

Chapter 1

Living in Feeling

When you see completely clearly – that is, when you see with a clear mind – then you find that the "I" is delusory and you can let go of it. It will go naturally – the mind won't hold on to it anymore. All things arise out of the unmanifest, therefore all things that have arisen have the unmanifest behind them, so when you see their true nature, you find that there is nothing. Therefore they must have been delusory.

You should bring mindfulness into daily life and give your full attention to everything you possibly can – but just one thing at a time. For example, you might be washing the dishes, then something else appears and demands your attention. Whatever it is, leave everything else and give your full attention to that, containing nothing else but that which is present. This is truly living in the moment, which has a great reality. You'll find that if you experience this, even if only for a few minutes, you feel completely safe – because you *are*, because there is nothing separate from you.

This is what mindfulness is – full of that object at that moment – not cluttered up with a lot of other things. It's coming out of you – not out of anyone else. You've found the true teacher – not out there, but inside you.

When you move beyond fear to a little more freedom, it begins to show itself for itself, by itself. It's almost as if there's something inside you unravelling and showing you who you really are. The only problem is you can't put an identity on it.

The Buddha talked about the apparent no-self, but he didn't talk about this. He talked about the conditioned self – the ego – but here there is the knowing that this is what I am. It is not an identity – not who I am, but what I am – a very subtle difference.

The physical body, the emotions and thought processes have to bow to this and begin to change – with nothing to be afraid of, you begin to feel more comfortable and at home. You find a unity inside yourself – head and heart come together as one. Each one begins to merge into the other, and there is oneness rather than separateness and fragmentation.

The intellect doesn't function in its own right – it becomes conditioned by feeling. When you look at your own intellectual processes, you find that to a degree they are very clinical and devoid of feeling. They are not personal but factual to themselves.

But when there is an opening in the heart area, feeling enters into it. The processes can't function clinically anymore. There is a new affinity between them and the objects of thought and so no more separation. All thought is separate from the thinker, but here you find that the thinker is one with thought. There is less abstract thought and a little more realisation, which doesn't require a lot of understanding anymore, because it has knowing in the sense of belonging in the feeling area, which is always united with things, whereas the intellect is always separate.

The intellect can't break into the feeling areas of oneness, but the feeling of oneness can break into the gaps and flow into the intellect, bringing it peace for the first time. If anything, it clarifies the whole process by eliminating an awful lot of repetition and unwanted mental activity. It thinks only when it needs to think. When it doesn't, there are spaces filled with perception and experience, moments of true contentment.

From time to time we all have thoughts that we don't want, which shows that there is a part of our minds which is always detached from thinking, which stands back and observes it. As we become clearer inside, a distance begins to open up between us and our thoughts. Gradually a space appears between thoughts – and meditation can help in this – and eventually thought is no longer automatic. We experience stillness. And this inner peace spreads to the people around us. People sense it when they're near you, and it spreads to them. You become a much more amenable companion; people become drawn to you, because you are still, never angry, never judgemental.

Thought is never true experience; it's a shadow of the real. This is where we come back to real things. What do you take as the real thing? The way you think about something or the way you feel about it? Feeling is the living process; thoughts deal with other things.

You can't consider the relationship between people as just a matter of information passing between them; it's based on a rapport. You feel this with your children and your partner; you don't have to think about it. But at the same time, it's not an emotional feeling, but rather a spreading out, absorbing feeling which becomes whatever you are experiencing, so that there is no separation.

You are living in feeling – not in the false world of abstraction which thought puts you in. You learn to sense-feel in a deeper way, not just emotionally, and you find that there is an extrasensory aspect to feeling which you aren't normally aware of. This means that you can take in a lot more experience, and that you can respond in a much better way, because there is a rapport. Thought always creates separation. But feeling brings union. In its deepest sense, it has a spiritual element, because it's unmanifest.

But contentment isn't something that we aim for. It's not a question of moving forward to a destination, but of dissociating ourselves from all the things that hold us back, whether you think of them as the seven deadly sins in Christianity or the hindrances in Buddhism. We make ourselves clearer – we allow our true selves to shine through, and contentment begins to emerge naturally.

We might feel a sense of something missing – but there's nothing missing from us. *We* are what is missing – from the whole. The whole is missing us.

We offer peace to others, the gift of peace. We don't shut anybody or anything out – we allow everything in. We absorb the world but we don't possess it. We become one with it.

Chapter 2

Pre-Birth, Birth and Childhood

I remember being born very vividly. It was more of a sensation, rather than thinking or identifying. I was in a darkish room and high up on the walls were long narrow windows, and there was gas lighting – though I obviously didn't know what it was at the time. It was painful to my eyes after being in the dark. The noise of the equipment being put down was shattering. I remember the sensation of the cool air after the warmth of the womb, taking it into my lungs, so it felt cold inside and outside. It was a devastating experience, emerging into all of that after the safety and warmth of the womb.

It was about 6.15 in the morning, on 29th June 1921. I was born in the Wellington Barracks in Victoria, at the back of Buckingham Palace. My father was a soldier, Sergeant Ambrose Harry Russel-Williams.

But I can remember even further back, before my birth. I've had glimpses of some of my previous lives. Mainly I remember the deaths rather than the lives. The first one I can remember very clearly is when I was living as a recluse in a promontory on the side of the mountain, which I realised was a volcano. There was a bit of a rumble every so often. I was living in a wooden hut, and had a broken leg. At some point I recall an eruption taking place and I lost consciousness then. It might have been Mount Vesuvius.

Another episode which intrigues me is when I was living in a cave in a mountain, pretty high up. The clothes I wore were distinctive – a woollen cloak, with black and white stripes about six inches wide. An avalanche took place and sealed the cave off and I died there. I've never found reference to that kind of robe anywhere even though I remember it very clearly.

In another life – or another death – I was running like mad across green grass towards a woodland, with horses thundering up behind me. There was a tremendous blow in the back so I assumed I'd been lanced. There was degree of fear which I haven't experienced in my present life.

My father was a wonderful friendly man, very easy to get along with. He was tall, 6 foot 1, dark hair and dark skinned, very thin. He had been a sergeant in the Coldstream Guards, and been gassed in the First World War, so his health was up and down. But he was an adaptable man, who could turn his hand to anything. Before I was 10, he'd taught me to cook and to repair a pair of shoes. He was musical, played the piano quite well and had a pleasant singing voice. He and my mother were both singers, around the piano, singing the songs of the day – *Come into the Garden, Maud, Wonderful Katie, I'll Be Waiting at the Kitchen Door, Burlington Bertie.*

He was strict, but also a very kindly man, always concerned about other people's well-being. There was one time when we were out in our car, an old blue Morris. I can still remember the number – NY 6993. We were going to Norfolk to visit some relatives who had a farm there. On the way, we passed a vehicle, a car that was stranded, stuck on the side of the road – it had run out of petrol. My dad used to carry a two-gallon can of petrol on the running board on the side of the car, and he gave it to this man. The man said, "Why don't I just take a bit of it and you keep the can?"

My dad said, "No, you keep it. And if you find someone else who's run out of petrol, give it to them."

Strangely, a similar thing happened to us three years later. We ran out of petrol and someone gave us a can – so we got it back.

My father loved nature. He'd grown up in the countryside near Guildford, and whenever possible, he would take us for walks in the countryside. He would show us flowers, plants, insects, and make us understand the natural world. We always had dogs and cats, and he was very caring to those as well.

My mother was from a large family in Essex, the Jones family. She was a gentle woman, very kindly, slightly built with wavy auburn hair. People would always take to her. My father met my mother's younger sister Dorothy first, during the First World War. She took him home, but when he met my mother, he fell for her. Her sister wasn't very happy about that, and it caused a few problems later on, after my mother died.

They had a good relationship, and between them they were charitable people, although we had very little. We were very poor, but we didn't know it, because we had a full life as an integrated family. That gave us a richness. In the 1920s work was very scarce, and my father would take whatever was available, which was why we kept moving around. That was why I went to so many different schools, 17 altogether.

I was the child in the middle, between my older brother and younger sister. My brother was 18 months older than me, my sister about 2 years younger. My brother was outgoing and I was more introverted. I didn't associate with other people. I felt more comfortable with animals. I always liked to be in the countryside, felt at home in nature, much more so than in man-made places. In my early years we were in a country setting, so I spent a lot of time exploring the fields with my dog. My dog and I were practically inseparable. I slept in the kennel with him. If I went missing, they would call the dog, because they knew I'd be there with him.

It was a happy existence – I was contented.

In this life I haven't experienced any fear. In the war I expected to be killed but I wasn't afraid. I was disturbed by the suffering I witnessed – soldiers' bodies torn apart, blown to pieces – but I was never afraid.

The first time I was aware of the lack of fear was when I was about five, when I was staying with my grandfather. Around that time, in the 20s, the NAAFI was formed – the Navy, Army and Air Force Institutes. The government set it up to cater for servicemen and their families overseas, to run the canteens and for recreation. My father applied for a job; he was accepted and posted to Egypt. At that time Egypt and Palestine were ruled by Britain. We didn't go with him straight away; we waited for a year or so, staying with my grandfather.

My grandfather was a larger than life character. He smoked about an ounce of tobacco a day and brewed his wines from herbs – elderberries, dandelions. He worked for the Wennington sand and gravel company, until he had to retire at 70. Then he took on a job as a labourer in a pit and went on till he was 80, loading wagons with a huge shovel. He had a plot of ground on the Southend Road, opposite the sand and gravel company. There were some old army Nissen huts, and he turned them into tearooms, which my grandmother ran. While we were staying there, to our amazement two elephants turned up one day, a grey one and a white, on their way to London Zoo. They were from the King of Siam – he was sending a white elephant as a present for the King of England, and they had brought a grey elephant too, to keep it company. They were walking from Tilbury docks, a good old trek, and they stayed overnight on my grandfather's plot, tethered up with wooden stakes in the corner.

Our dog Tinker ran out and started barking at the elephants. That made one of them angry – it coiled up its trunk, lifted up Tinker and threw him into the air. I dashed up to the elephant and pummelled its legs with my fists. The elephant wrapped its trunk around me and lifted me into the air, and put me down again. The adults were horrified, but I didn't feel any fear at all, just anger that my dog had been thrown.

Soon after that my mother and us three kids sailed out to Heliopolis. My father was running supplies for the whole of the area, British-administered Egypt and Palestine. I went to school in Heliopolis for a while, then we were moved into Palestine. I remember the train journey very well – it was so slow and rickety that every now and then we got out and walked alongside it, just to get some exercise. It took about 30 hours. We were put into a compound of civilians in a place called Sarafand, about 20 miles inland from Jaffa – near Tel Aviv – near to the RAF base in Ramallah. That was where I went to school. It was close to where St George was buried, after his death in the Crusades.

During that time my mother got seriously ill. She picked up congestion of the lungs and was taken up to a sanatorium in Lebanon. Dad used to borrow a car and drive up there once a month to see her. It was around that time that I had a powerful realisation, at the age of nine. Because my mother was away and we were on our own so much, I was doing the cooking, preparing food for lunch, looking after the house, looking after my sister. I thought about my mother and how hard our lives were and it occurred to me that there was something strange about all the suffering I was witnessing. I knew there was physical suffering but this was deeper than that, and I was sure there had to be a reason for it, even though it was beyond my understanding at the time. I was determined that one day I would find out what it was.

I didn't even have the opportunity to think about it and try to understand it until much later. We moved about so much, and life was such a struggle – especially after my parents died – that there wasn't any time to do anything but keep going.

One odd thing about my childhood was the number of times I came close to death, every time through nearly drowning. When I look back at my life, it's as if I've not been allowed to die. When I was about two years old, we were walking along the side of the River Thames at Richmond with some relatives. I tripped up and took a nosedive into the river, head first. My uncle grabbed hold of my ankles as I went in, and pulled me out. I barely remember it, but they told me the only dry bit left on me was the soles of my feet.

The second time was when I was four years old. We were living near the River Brent in Northolt, which was normally just a trickle. But there had been heavy rain and it was flooded. Again, I tripped and fell in, and this time my dog Tinker pulled me out, grabbed me between his teeth and dragged me to safety. We both arrived home drenched to the bone.

Later, in Palestine we used to go swimming at a beach just outside Jaffa, Campbell's Cove we called it, a small bay on the Mediterranean. On three different occasions, I was caught in an undertow and dragged out to sea. Coincidentally, it was the same policeman who pulled me out each time, a friend of my father's. The last time I remember him carrying me out, my dad was there, and the policeman shouted to him, "Harry! It's about time you taught this little bugger to swim!"

I was well aware that I could have died but I wasn't concerned. There was no panic or pain, just quiet acceptance. I remember thinking, "If that's the way it's going to be, so be it."

Around 1931, the troubles started in Palestine, when Jews started arriving from Europe. We lived in a compound outside the military area, between an Arab village and a Jewish settlement. There was no trouble between them; they got on fine. We would go into Tel Aviv, a mainly Jewish place, and then into Jaffa, which was mainly Arab, but there was very little disharmony between the two peoples. But then there was an exodus of Jews from Russia, trying to fight their way in. The army decided it was unsafe, so we were all evacuated out of it, and came home.

I went back to school in London, and my dad had a temporary job with the City of London police reserve, in the canteen. By this time, his health was deteriorating, due to the effects of being gassed, and someone fixed him up with a job which they thought would suit him better, in Coventry. He became the steward of the Triumph Motor Sports club, on Binley Road, opposite one of the

Triumph factories. It was a huge place, even though it was just a one-storey building. There was a dance hall cum theatre, four snooker tables, a room for playing cards, and at the back end there was a huge plunge pool for people who played football and rugby. Outside there was a 9-hole golf course, and four tennis courts.

We were only there a year or two when my dad died. It must have been partly to do with being out on the golf course in all extremes of weather, mowing the lawns of the golf course in the cold – he caught a cold which turned into pneumonia which eventually led to pleurisy. He died in King George's Hospital in Warwick, aged 42. I was just 10.

They let us stay at the sports club for a year or so, then we had to move into rented accommodation in Coventry. My mother was trying to keep us afloat, working as a baths attendant in the daytime and a barmaid in a pub in the night time, trying to earn enough to keep the family together. She was a gentle person so it was brutal to see her work so hard, to watch her wear herself out like that, suffering from consumption at the same time.

Around this time my brother George was 12 years old and decided to join the Navy, in the boy's service. That took a bit of the burden away from my mother, and he gained a very good education through that, and eventually spent his whole life in the Navy – 35 years before he retired. The British Legion helped us by giving my mother a 10 shilling a week pension, although it didn't help that much because she was in a very poorly state, almost too ill to work.

I insisted I should go to work to help out. There were some friends of the family trying to help us out, but in those days there was hardly any money around. Someone suggested I should become an apprentice to a printer, but there was no point going to work for no pay as an apprentice because we needed money. We got special dispensation from the council to allow me to leave school. I was about 11 and a half, so I went to work in an engineering factory in Coventry. It was rough work, clearing away the cuttings from the lathes. They were razor sharp, and I had to pick them out of the rubbish with my bare hands. It wasn't pleasant, believe you me. And they only paid me 10 shillings a week.

The factory was at the bottom of a hill in Gulson Road. There was a hospital at the other end of the road – and that was where my mother died, about 18 months after my father.

When my father died I was quite content, because somehow I knew that death was not the end, and I knew he was still around, and in a better place. And I felt the same with my mother. I sensed it – I was aware of the exact moment when she died, at about three o'clock in the afternoon, while I was at the factory. I was happy for her too, because I knew she was clear; I knew she was free of suffering. It left a big hole, a big sense of loss, but I knew it was for the best.

That day, I returned home to our little two-up, two-down terraced house, and my grandfather was there, with two of my mother's younger sisters. As I walked up to the door, one of the sisters opened it in my face and blurted out, "Your mother's dead" – as direct as that, in a very brutal way. And I just said, "I know." They had already been through the whole house, looting anything that was of value.

Since my brother was already in the Navy, he was fine. The problem was my sister who was barely nine years old. I found out later that she didn't even remember her mother. She was taken in by my grandmother, who placed her with my mother's next youngest sister. But I insisted on being on my own, because I knew what kind of people they were, and I didn't want to deal with them. My grandfather on my mother's side did try to get me into Barnardo's – the children's home – but at that time they wouldn't take children my age.

After they died, I was desperate, and virtually half-starved. I was very frustrated. Not so much because of their deaths – I knew they weren't really dead anyway; once or twice I even sensed their presence. But without them to support me life was very hard. I took digs with a friend and his family, but 10 shillings a week was nowhere near enough to live on, so I did part-time jobs in the evening. It was exhausting – six days a week, all the hours from morning till bedtime. On Sunday I'd just spend the whole day flat out on my bed, exhausted. It was just an existence, not a life.

In the course of one of my part-time jobs, collecting glasses in a pub just for a couple of extra bob – a pot man, they called it – I met a chap who told me I'd be better off going to Hull to work on a trawler. You'll get the clothing you need for the job, he said, you'll get fed and have somewhere to sleep. I thought, "That sounds better than this life." So I hitchhiked my way across to Hull, and I found a job on a trawler called the *Dungeness*. I was only about 12 and a half at the time, but I'd had my employment card stamped. The captain didn't care how I old was anyway, as long as I could do what was necessary.

For some reason – maybe because there was some overfishing going on, or too many boats – they decided to take a run up into the Arctic. Besides the skipper, there were five of us crewmembers. We would trawl for about four hours at a time, before hauling in the load of fish, then rest for about an hour and a half before we did the next trawl. This went on around the clock – we couldn't take a night's sleep until we were back at the shore. Normally people would be out for just a few days, but we were out for about a month.

It was winter, so it was very unpleasant. We had a few storms, with waves as high as this house. There was one dangerous situation when we took shelter in the lee side of an island. The snow was building up and freezing up; we had to take axes to chip it off the rigging, otherwise we would have turned turtle, capsized. Rope that was as thick as your wrist became a foot wide. But again, I felt no fear. I accepted the situation and did my best to help alleviate it. I didn't feel any emotional pain; just the physical discomfort of being cold and tired.

We got back with a full load of fish – cod, halibut, you name it. We returned to port, unloaded the fish and they were taken to market. The other crewmembers were coaling up, pulling up the winch to lift the coal. The deck was wet, and one of the crew slipped and was about to fall on to the winch. I pulled him away, but got hooked up on it myself. I was hospitalized, with several fractures in my right hand and arm, and that was the end of my time on the trawler.

After a few weeks my money was all used up, and I decided that the best idea was to head back to London, a bigger place with more opportunity. I worked my way down, on a few farms, harvesting potatoes – it was done by hand in those days, backbreaking work. In London I did a few menial jobs – at the dirty end of everything, the lowest possible things, just to survive. Portering, humping sacks of potatoes and swedes at Spitalfields market, frying doughnuts in a bakery. I had no education behind me – we'd moved around so much during my childhood that I'd never had the chance to settle in at any school. I was a boy without a place in life, in total desperation, with no thought other than keeping myself alive. There was no enjoyment in life whatsoever.

Eventually someone advised me to go to the Salvation Army working lads' hostel. They put me up, looked after me and found me a better job. That's how I came to work with one Benjamin Shapiro, a Jewish man. He was a Polish refugee from the previous war – the First World War – who was running a little tailors' outfit, manufacturing ladies' coats and mantles for the big shops in London. He was a very kindly gentleman – I remember him with great affection.

I worked with him for a couple of years. He started me off on 30 shillings a week – a pretty good wage for the time – and after a year or so he gave me a rise to 2 pounds. I was a general factotum, as you might say. I'd hire a barrow for sixpence, a costermonger's barrow, and we'd fill it with bundles of clothes in wrappers, and I'd take them off to the big stores, to the back doors. And there was a checker who would go through each piece of clothing meticulously, while I was there. I had to have a needle and thread, in case something needed repairing.

I'd been there only about six weeks, making these weekly trips to big stores in London, when Mr Shapiro asked me to collect his cheques on Saturdays. I had to cash them and then take the money over to his house in Stepney. In retrospect, I can't believe he trusted me with all that money after just six weeks. When I took the money back to his house, I would put it all on the mantelpiece – he wouldn't touch it until the Sunday, because it was the Sabbath. I worked on Saturdays and they worked on Sundays. I'd arrive about lunchtime and his wife would give me a cold meal – she didn't cook on Saturdays, of course. It was very pleasant. For the first time in my life, things seemed to be getting a little easier.

Then the war came along.

Chapter 3

The Nature of Consciousness

Emptiness

If you endeavour to construct knowledge of what you're trying to seek, you close the door to the actual experience. The only way to attain the experience is to come to a complete emptiness of the thought-mind: total emptiness. And if one dwells there for any length of time, then one begins to find that the emptiness was never empty because it contains the potential for all that may come to be. We enter into an area of extremely fine aspects of consciousness that, dissolving into itself, loses duality. And there is only that.

If you take anything that is manifest, sentient or insentient, and look deeply into its nature, you find that it has the same nature of consciousness. There are so many things which have a truth about them. In Buddhism we have the unborn, the unmanifest, the uncreated – and out of that come the created and the manifest. Biblically, we have a similar thing in Genesis – in the beginning there is but void, out of which comes the so-called word. This is the vibratory aspect, out of which comes the world.

But all leads back to the emptiness – the no-thing from which the something arises. No form of understanding can connect you to this. It has to be seen within itself. It's way beyond understanding. The peace that passeth understanding – that is the emptiness. This is completely fulfilling in itself. After suffering from delusion through many lifetimes, we find the truth.

You can't explain it to anybody. It's not me doing it anymore – it's just the body going through its processes. You do think when you need to think, but you find that thoughts arise by themselves. Who's thinking them? Or do they just arise using the same process you would use if you wanted to think? Are you really thinking all your thoughts or are they just passing through? Most of the time it's just repetition, passing through, completely unnecessary.

You can just be instead of think. Unless you specifically want to think of something that's useful, it's just a habitual process which goes on inside our heads. Positive thought is one thing – irrational thought is another. A lot of the time we think things we don't want to think, so who's in control?

When this happens, ignore the thought and go down into the feeling area. Gradually this brings some control, the ability to think when you want to, and to not think when you don't need to.

Sometimes thoughts have such a powerful momentum.

The way to curtail that is to move from thought into feeling. The mind has to be active, never still. If it turns from thinking into feeling, even in the sense of feeling nothing, it is still aware. It is still doing something even when there's no activity.

Consciousness can become still – but it doesn't *think* it is still; it just knows it. When you examine the nature of the mind at stillness, it's actually very energetic – a contradiction in terms. The stillness which is so-called silence can be very active, because of all the energy it contains.

If you examine the Buddhist term mindfulness from the point of experience, you find that you cannot be mindful unless the mind is empty. Mindfulness means being full of that which is there – and if it is full of this, it cannot contain anything else. Concepts and ideas have to go. There is only that. Mind-ful-ness. In the moment, this experience is all there is.

Mind is pure consciousness. Not being conscious of thinking, that is something different. Thinking is just a process, not the mind itself. Mind is that which observes the thinking, not that which does it. "I think therefore I am" – it's only true in the sense of "I think therefore I am an ego self." Otherwise it's completely wrong.

You can only think in terms of duality. Duality creates ego-consciousness; duality is always unsatisfactory. There should ideally be total oneness – anything else is fragmented. I think therefore I am an ego – not the deeper level of I am. Realisation does not require identification.

Then we come to the point where that which sees, knows only insight. It sees it within, not out there, because it sees the nature thereof. And this nature can only be known by its own expression within.

I'm realising more and more how consciousness knows, if we just let it come out and do it for itself.

That's right. Consciousness is spirit. Unless there is feeling, there is no understanding. When you learn to feel, then you have understanding and can work with it, but if it is just 'upstairs', it's just confusion. Feeling is the key to appreciating consciousness because consciousness only knows things through feeling, whether it be coarsely, or extremely finely, or anything in between. It only knows feeling.

It's good to learn to allow feeling to take place, in the sense of being conscious, rather than demanding to see or know something. If you just look at a seemingly blank wall, a blank wall is all you see, but if you quietly gaze at it without anything in mind, you'll see a lot of little impressions in the wall which you never knew existed. When you are just conscious, it will show itself to you, as other things will show their nature to you. If you *demand* something, you'll only get what you demand and it won't be what is really there. If you truly give your full attention – and I mean *full* attention – to another person, if only for a second or so, without any thought at all, you'll find you give *yourself* to that person. There is only that person, and he or she will blossom in that moment, through your attention. In the seeing there is only that which is seen. So if you are without concepts or ideas, you see things truly for what they are.

It's almost as if suffering is a result of the conflict between thought and feeling.

It is. Thought means moving away from being truly conscious of things, moving away into ideas, into separation. It doesn't work. This is why a person who lives in empathy will pick up other people's feelings very easily, their troubles as well as their joys, and experience precisely what they're going through; not necessarily their thoughts, and not necessarily wholly their emotions, but they will come to know *them*, as people. In that way, you come to understand other people, and accept them for what they are.

There was a philosopher who said the mind is nothing apart from its contents – perceptions, thoughts and impressions.

A very confused statement. You can't look into mind because you are mind and mind is both inside and outside in terms of consciousness. In many ways we only know the world around us – or the universe for that matter – in terms of seeing it as a reflection of our inner world. We don't see it as reality; it's just a screen on which we project our world. Different people see different things at the same time. If you go outside on a clear night and see thousands of stars you can sense-feel them within yourself, for that is your nature. It's not separate from you. All that's between you is space – and that space is consciousness. That's your nature. That is consciousness – it's in here, not out there.

One area we can't translate with any accuracy is communicating with one another, particularly in the area of affection. A touch will do that, or a glance, but words are inadequate. It's done without thought. How do you communicate with a baby – with words or with feeling? We just do things naturally in the feeling area.

Words are useful to some degree because they hold the attention, and once they are being used, a sense-feeling emerges which is absorbed. That is really what translates the words into something which really matters. How do you record that?

There's just the experience of this moment, which you can't record. They're the things that make the difference.

The real trick about all this is to learn to be completely open at times. Not all the time – there are times when you need to be closed, particularly out there in the world. But if you can be more open in certain areas, you find you can begin to experience the nature of one another. You attune your own nature to that, and after this you begin to get a different view of the whole world. It doesn't mean to say that you exchange thoughts, but you share the same nature. You begin to appreciate the wholeness of things rather than the separateness, either with animals, people or plants. This doesn't require thought or identity – it's just the very nature of being itself. This is a very strange thing in many ways – because on the one hand it means a sense of holiness, a sense of the way things ought to be. On the other hand, it means a sense of nurturing or becoming its true nature.

Wholeness, becoming, further nurturing into further wholeness – it doesn't make sense in words, but that is the real nature we're dealing with. When we get moments of silence in groups such as this, when we allow thoughts to fade away and become aware of a greater expansiveness – there's a very comfortable warmth, which you wish you could remain within. It's a wordless experience, a knowing of rightness.

Consciousness as the Unmanifest

What is the nature of consciousness?

It is the unmanifest area, and that is why it is in everything and can know everything. It is what some people call God. Religions say that God made the world, but I disagree wholeheartedly. We use the word God for the true consciousness, the universal consciousness. Call it God if you wish, but God is not an entity. It is not a superhuman being. It is merely consciousness. Now if everything has emanated out of this, there is every reason why consciousness can be known from any part to another part, be it animate or inanimate. It can still be known within consciousness because it is the manifestation of consciousness itself.

Consciousness is far more than it appears to be, so in actual fact I am part of you. It's what we are sharing at this moment. We are sharing this experience. How can you or I be separate, other than physically? There is a manifestation here, and the part in between us is the part that is manifested. That is the part that is experiencing.

Yet this is very ordinary.

Oh, this is perfectly ordinary, yes! It is happening all the time with everybody, and they don't even know it. It's a different level of consciousness that sees it, different to the normal so-called world consciousness, which is too dumb and coarse to see it.

You said a while ago that one never feels a particular age.

We are universally young and becoming, not getting old and dying, though the body is aging. If you cling wholly to the physical, you might feel that you are dying, that your body is aging, getting weaker, and you will obviously pass and leave this world. But the consciousness is still young and it is not concerned or afraid. It senses that when death occurs it will be released.

From the point of being born into the world, the body starts aging and replacing itself: the nails, the hair, the skin cells slough off all the time. So there is a physical death and rebirth process going on all the time. The body now is not the same entity that came into the world, or even what it was 10 years ago.

It is inevitable that all that comes to be will also fade away – the Buddha was right in this. Sentient life obviously has a shorter lifespan than that which is insentient. The average person assumes that the aging of the body is the aging of themselves, but when you awaken the consciousness a little, you realise that you are not your body. Yes, the body is aging, and ultimately will fade away, but that which is observing, the conscious entity, knows it will not die. It is eternal. There is no death for that. Death is only for the physical. This is why people who have had some experience of things of a spiritual nature are not afraid of dying – because they know it gives release from the imprisonment of the physical body. The body *is* a prison – you're stuck with it until you die. But you can reach a higher level of consciousness which doesn't need to come back to the physical to learn any lessons through it.

You can speak of physical experiences, or semi-physical experiences, but there is nothing you can say of the spirit. If you go past the physical, you have no identity to speak of, therefore no separation. There has to be a degree of manifestation and separation in order for us to communicate from one to another. You can only communicate what another could experience. If there is nobody there experiencing, how can experience be communicated? There is nobody to communicate and nobody there to communicate to either.

Emotions may arise – the body may change its chemistry, it may heat up or cool down, but does it affect me? Have you ever experienced anger building up until you feel you could murder somebody, and yet you're quietly sitting there thinking, "What the hell is going on here?" It's not you, it is a conditioned happening. Conditioned happening becomes identified as a so-called self which isn't there. We think that because this is happening there must be somebody doing it – a self, an ego, a burden. When we realise that consciousness is what we are, all of this conditioning means nothing. It doesn't lead anywhere, so we can just let it go, and it will die out. Then we become more peaceful. Because peace is the nature of consciousness. It never gets upset. It just reveals facets of itself to itself and sees them as conditioning.

Does the conditioning have deep roots?

It starts with an identification with our physical existence. We become aware of these things as we progress. The trouble is we try to understand them, and we can't. You try to put it into verbal understanding and it won't fit. Forget the understanding; just know: this is the way things are. Just accept that.

It is a question of seeing a paradox, putting the two sides of the paradox together as one, and accepting both, not in opposition but as complementary. In a paradoxical situation, both left and right are equally right at their own level, but that which sees it is in the middle and is neither one nor the other. It does not take sides any more, for it can accept both.

A strange thing about being in the physical body is that its most important aspect is the blood. Without blood, the body cannot maintain itself. But what is it that the blood carries around as it services the body? Oxygen. So in actual fact gas in a liquefied form is being carried around the body. And is not gas closest to emptiness? This body is just a gasbag *(laughs)*. How could it not know the emptiness, since it is filled with gas, and with space? They say the body is mostly made up of water, and what is water but H2O? Two gases.

So the body is something and nothing. Why do we place such importance on it? We don't, strictly speaking – rather, we place importance on the activities that take place within it, which is a different thing altogether. The living aspect is not physical at all. It's the interplay between this and other things that is important. If I am in interplay with that tree or that house or that chimneypot over there, am I here or over there? Am I here in my consciousness or over there in your consciousness? It's an intriguing question, because there is an element of yes, and no. It is and it isn't.

So what can we really be sure about? Not a lot, and if we just accept it as it appears, there is no problem. But if we try to analyse it, we fall into difficulties. So why not just accept it? This is one of those little aspects of experience that only happen for a moment. You cannot deny your experience because that is your reality, so be careful what you experience. It is your only truth.

Words are not true – they can be disproved. But you cannot disprove experience any more than you can prove it to be true *(laughs)*. It does not go away, because you cannot stop the world. You can try to stop the world so you can understand it, but you find that it's already moving on.

Who am I?

When I try to observe what and who I am, it's as if there are different levels. There are thoughts on a superficial level, and concepts of who I think I am from my past.

Yes, and you can sense that these are not the real you. Why don't you believe that? It's telling you the truth. You are not a self. If you have to cling to something, there has to be a self, otherwise there is nothing else.

The point is that you're looking at these aspects with duality, rather than singularly. If you give full attention to any one aspect there is only that. If you give full attention to me, where does your self go? You know this now, because there is only this. If I give you attention there is only you and not me. If the mind is full of 'that' there is no me looking. That is true experience. Is it possible that consciousness and experience exist together, and other than that there is nothing?

This fits with the speculation that things must be as they are now.

When you say "as they are now", the now has already gone *(laughs)*. You stand still and everything passes you by, or perhaps everything is stationary and you pass it by. It's like a vehicle heading down the road at whatever speed you like, but there is always the stationary aspect of the tyre in contact with the road, without which the car would be skidding. But it's so rapid that you don't notice. There is always that still moment – the moment of contact, of experience. The now. If you can live in that now you have no problems. No maybes, no maybe-nots, only now.

How is it that some people are able to pass on this sort of knowledge, both verbally or through feeling?

Just through their nature. It depends on whether they consider it important enough to do so, or whether they feel they can do it accurately enough. You can experience a lot of things which are impossible to explain to another person, or even to yourself. This is the very thing that makes the Buddha outstanding in history – the manner in which he was able to observe within himself aspects of grasping, jealousy, hatred and other characteristics, and to explain where they come from and how to deal with them. He was able to elucidate these phenomena absolutely clearly and precisely, and that is quite unique. Yes, others have come after him, but they haven't achieved this to the same degree.

Some people have the ability to translate between different realms, which others cannot do. I'm not so proficient at this – I can give you the experience so that you can sense it, but I can't explain it in words as the Buddha did. I can bring about a rapport and a feeling so that you can begin to appreciate what it means. But that's not the same as explaining it by rote.

As you read various books, not the history of Buddhism, but about the lives of various teachers, my observation is that the better ones seem to operate much like this.

Yes. A transmission takes place from experience to experience. But the Buddha explained things so clearly that they could be put down for others to read. I couldn't do that, not a chance – I'm not academic in the least! *(Laughs.)* But I find I can draw people together and produce a situation in which they can sense and understand things and appreciate them in their own experience. This is the only real way I can communicate. So it is experience talking to experience, rather than word to word, or intellect to intellect. And so transmission does take place, sometimes more rapidly than you might think. But it is not deliberate, it just happens.

When we absorb things from one another, it's because we're familiar with who we're dealing with. The same thing can happen at a deeper level through association. This is what Sangha is: achieving a rapport, finding a level of togetherness, which means communication can take place without words.

Anybody who has begun to stir the conscious aspects within themselves will be able to notice or pick up quite a lot of phenomena from incidents that happen around them, and will begin to appreciate them directly without any form of understanding. However, you have to open up the consciousness a little more than normal. This could happen accidentally or deliberately. Where it is deliberate, the opening of consciousness is carried over into other situations. Then you may begin to see more, in depth, and that is where you can keep it.

Shared Consciousness

I feel as if there is a compass inside that takes me here and there but is not visible. That is what I associate with the word 'spirit'.

Yes, that inner compass is there. When you really experience it, when you are *in* it, although you've gone inside to find it, it is neither inside nor outside, but both. It seems to go beyond the body. You suddenly find that it's out here. It does not have any measure; it is bigger than the void.

Spirit is the only word you can put on it. Spirit is the mysterious so-called substance that isn't a substance, which is not physical and yet is very much physical. This is what we might call presence.

Here we are looking back to the unconditioned, the unborn, the unmanifest, in Buddhist terms. But when you come to weigh it up, it's as big as the Universe itself. It is Consciousness. It operates through the physicality of the brain. When we begin to appreciate it for what it really is then we find it is nothing to do with the body whatsoever, although in some fashion it is attached to the body in this physical world. But it's *only* attached to it. It is never part of the physical body at all, and it operates outside the body as well as inside it.

Whilst we are within the body we sense things inside it which are outside. That may sound strange, but at certain times – particularly with somebody you are close to, even a dog or a cat – you might have a feeling that something is wrong. Then you investigate and find that your feeling was true. How do you know? Do they reach out to you, or do you reach out to them, or are you both the one? You can't define it. But since the sensation is there and since it is proven to be true, consciousness knows it, even though we have to translate it into words.

So there is a shared consciousness through which we can transmit and pick up information?

Yes, but in the sharing we find that consciousness is compartmentalised, to you, or me, or somebody else, and becomes attached to your conditioning, which is different to mine, so that you appear to have an individual consciousness. You can think in terms of a light that sees all things, which is unchanging. The light is there to see, and we individually see our own, but we don't see someone else's.

Consciousness never thinks, it's impossible for it to think, therefore it can never identify. It cannot therefore be individual in the sense of this or that; it has to be universal. But in our limited situation, because the body is the dense material through which consciousness is working, it's like looking through a thick blanket. You can't see very much light, and we're stuck with our own experiences, which we believe are reality. But the light sees all, and when we can achieve a complete rapport with another person, the self no longer exists. There is only the other one. Then consciousness can act both ways at the same time. There is no person there and you experience the same as the other.

This is the most interesting part of the whole process, learning the nature of consciousness itself, which knows through both the crudest and the most subtle areas of feeling. Consciousness doesn't think, it doesn't identify, it just knows by experience. Therefore it doesn't know time, it only knows now. What is happening now is all. It doesn't have to think about it. The now is constantly moving on, so it does not carry memories.

With scents and smells, we can have very coarse ones or very fine ones, all of different natures, but it's very difficult to quantify the whole range of them. Some are very faint, almost non-existent, yet still we pick them up; and if you are familiar with them, you can identify them. If not, you wonder what they are, and tell yourself, "I don't know what that one is." But this all takes place in the most sensitive areas of feeling. Similarly, consciousness will pick up all kinds of things, and you may not even be aware of them. Consciousness even operates beyond the range of the physical. It communicates by feeling: we feel that things are pleasant or positive; we feel things are negative. But where in the body do we feel them? Do we feel them in the body, or in the space within the body?

The space within the body is not an organ. It's not the body itself experiencing, but consciousness. There are some things consciousness does through the body, and other things it does without the body. In the sensitive areas, it operates without the body; in the coarser areas it operates with the body. So it would appear that the nature of the consciousness itself lies mainly within the finer aspects rather than the coarser, because it needs the physical body to know the coarser aspects. This seems to be the case, although it's only an observation, which may be true or false. But you can see it for yourselves if you look.

The space within the body doesn't have to be big. It can be as small as a pinhead, and still be quite adequate because it's part of a whole universe of space.

Death and Birth

I feel as if I'm evolving gradually towards a more spiritual state, but everybody I know about who has become enlightened or realised seems to have had a sudden dramatic experience, some kind of crisis. Do you think that is always the case?

I wouldn't say that necessarily. It may appear that way; but generally speaking, people have had experiences in previous lives which have brought them to this point. Even in this life there's usually a period when they have concentrated intensely for a long period of time. In my own case, there were three years, day and night, looking after animals – a whole mindful process for a long period. Ramana* had a few years. He had a glimpse when he tried to experience death, but it still took another 10 years. He was about 27 when he finally became awakened. It's not just sudden – the previous lives make a difference. A lot of work takes place in the past, before we come into this lifetime. In my case, I knew this was my last time around. I wasn't even looking for enlightenment this time around, which seems to be the right way when I look back on it.

The only thing you can do to prepare the way is to clear the mind. It's no good trying to think and understand it. It won't work. What you have to do is to train yourself to be more fully aware of what you're doing. That's why I instruct people to put their mind in their hands and be consciously aware. Let your hands tell you what you want to do rather than the other way around. Do this and your mind will gradually clear. And when you reach the stage where you virtually have a clear mind, there is the chance of something arising. It's within you already. It's your own nature in the first place. As long as you're not concerned about where you're going, just what you're doing now – now as in a physical feeling rather than a mental – you'll find that awareness will take you to deeper levels, much more subtle areas where you can observe your emotions without getting involved. Then you see the nature of the mind, how concepts are formed and how they disappear.

Emptiness is the key – the clear, empty mind. Whatever you observe becomes the whole content of the mind. You gain access into a totally new dimension from which all these things arise. In Buddhist terms, this is the unborn, uncreated, unmanifest which is the essence of everything. You can observe the whole world arising – a very interesting process. You can see the falsity and the delusory duality in it, and the manifestations of different forms of the same thing.

And yet we are so afraid of losing this form. It seems to be part of being human to be afraid of death.

There is nothing to be afraid of; it's just like going into the next room. The manner of dying may be painful, or perhaps people are afraid of losing the idea of self – they may think it means annihilation. I sometimes wonder if it's not fear of death, but fear of birth which is the problem. Birth is a very traumatic experience – as I remember myself. An innate memory may be there, that death leads to birth, which creates fear.

The strange thing is that these feelings are felt and known without any thought whatsoever: in relation to birth, there is a consciousness that dawns in a dark, warm place, a place that is caressing, with the mother's blood flow and pulse. This is absolute comfort. But then for no apparent reason there is a pressure squeezing you in. Imagine a boa constrictor trying to constrict you, turning you around and upside down and eventually squeezing you through a narrow tube, like a one-foot-sized ball being pushed through a six-inch pipe. You've been breathing like a fish with gills, in liquid, and you come out all wet, into a cold atmosphere after being immersed in warm water. Suddenly there's light after dark. After muffled noise, somebody suddenly drops something on to a tin plate, making a loud clang, and somebody grabs you by the feet and yanks you up and pulls the liquid out of you so that you breathe cold air into a warm lung, like breathing in cold air first thing in the morning... And all of this at the same time. It's painful – the whole process of birth is pain. The womb is completely safe, but out here you are totally exposed, in a hostile world.

So I wonder if that is part of the fear of death, that it leads to rebirth. But of course this memory is innate; people don't really know it consciously. It is the deeper levels of consciousness that know it.

Death is a process of each of the senses gently and quietly closing down. It depends on the person, how spiritually developed they are, but in perhaps a few days they're in another dimension. The average person shouldn't have any great difficulty, although less developed people may have some. Once I was knocked up at three o'clock in the morning because a person was dying in a terrible way. I got dressed and went into their bedroom, lit a candle and it was like being in hell. She was absolutely tormented, within and without. On the surface she was a perfectly ordinary person, but she had a weak mind, and had attracted negative forces, primeval forces which are always looking for a point of entry into the physical world. It took me two hours to clear it out, and finally she died in a more stable state.

Generally speaking though, you don't need to worry about it – those who are spiritually advanced are automatically protected. Most people will die in a parallel world to this, where there is less pressure of conditioning. Even though there are conditions, it won't take them long to discover what form their next life is going to take, and then they will be born again. More advanced people will make an assessment of the situation themselves, and will be able to decide on the kind of entry they require.

Note
* Ramana Maharshi, the Indian spiritual teacher with whom Russel feels strongly connected (see Chapters 12 and 14).

Chapter 4

The War

I remember it quite clearly. It was a brilliant sunny day, a Sunday. I was walking along Bow Road, and a policeman came along on a bicycle, shouting out, "The country's at war! The country's at war! The prime minister will speak at 11 o'clock!" We knew the war was coming, of course. We were even surer of it than the government.

At first we just carried on as usual. I put my name down for the local defence force – which later became the home guard – but nothing happened for a while. Then in January 1940, I volunteered for the army, and was enrolled overnight. It was a shock – I didn't realise it would happen so quickly. I was living in Bow, in Brick Lane, which was all Jewish in those days. I enrolled in Hammersmith, which was the other side of London. I was given 24 hours to clear out my things and get into uniform. Mr Shapiro gave me his blessing, and off I went.

I arrived at Hammersmith with about 30 others. We were taken round to a local depot to be kitted out with a uniform, a spare uniform, three sets of underwear, socks and boots. The last thing they gave us was a steel helmet and a rifle. The sergeant asked, "Does anyone know how to use this?" pointing at the rifle.

"Yes," I replied. When I was a kid there were a lot of guns around, especially in Palestine, and my father, like a lot of army people, had thought it would be wise to teach us how to use them, so we didn't have accidents.

"Go and stand over there."

There were about four of us. The other 25 or so disappeared – we never saw them again. We were marched up to Wormwood Scrubs, alongside the prison, on to a firing range. We had to fire shots on to a target and then clean our weapons to prove that we could use them. Then we were taken to what had been a Territorial Army base on Goldhawk Road in Shepherds Bush. We went on duty straight away, without any training whatsoever. We were taken out to various vulnerable points around the city – London Docks, the marshalling yards at the railways at Harlesden, the Central Telegraph Office. Our job was to look out for saboteurs, anyone who might try to sabotage the transport or communication systems. We were supposed to challenge anyone we didn't know, with the power to shoot them.

Then I became a company runner – it was my job to keep in contact with the various platoons out in different areas. If communications were lost, I would travel about, from one platoon to another, delivering food, passing messages. If anyone was ill, I had to take their place.

This went on for weeks – on duty, off duty. Once I got used to it, I enjoyed being a soldier. It saved me from a bad end, kept me out of trouble – and most importantly, it took away the worry of keeping myself alive. I had regular food and shelter for the first time since my parents died. It was easy, compared to the life I had before. It also taught me self-discipline, to control my emotions.

In May 1940 I got a 48-hour pass. It was a beautiful day, and I decided to visit my mother's eldest sister, in Tooting, South London. I hadn't seen her for years but I knew where she lived. As it was such a nice day, I thought I'd walk over the river and then take a tram. But I never got to my aunt's. As I was walking along Westminster Bridge, there was a little jetty along the side, near the Houses of Parliament, and I saw a boat tied up there. I'd been working at the docks and I knew that pleasure boats weren't allowed on the river anymore. So I jumped over the gate – which was locked – and went to see what was going on.

There was a man on the boat working on the engine. "What are you doing here?" I said to him. "You shouldn't be on the river with that."

"It's okay," he said. "A radio call came in at midnight, asking anybody with a boat over 28 feet long to bring them down to Chatham as fast as possible. We don't know why. My engine's conked out. I've got an oil line that's clogged."

I helped him clear it out and offered to go down there with him.

We went down to Chatham and discovered what it was all about: the evacuation of Dunkirk. We were towed out at midnight, through the Thames Estuary and out into the Channel. The destroyers and the other big ships couldn't get to the beaches, they had to have at least a 12-foot depth of water to manoeuvre, and the sea at Dunkirk was shallow, like Southport.

They took us to a particular point over the Channel, and then let us loose, to head towards the beaches. The original idea was for proper sailors to take over the boats, but the chap I was with said, "Let us do it – we know how the boat works. It makes more sense for us to do it." Some people let sailors take over their boats, some didn't.

"You'll be fine," they told us. "It's perfectly fine – there's no danger. Away you go."

By that time it was nearly daylight – dawn just breaking. We came in closer, maybe 5 or 6 miles out, and we saw what looked like piers, one after the next, from one end of the beach to the other, jutting out into the sea. We thought we must have come to the wrong place, but as we moved closer we discovered that they weren't piers – they were lines of men, standing up to their waists in the water. They were expecting us. We arrived at the end of one of these lines of men, and there was a sergeant waiting for us.

"How many can you take?"

I said, "I don't know – just keep loading until we're full."

The next thing I knew, wounded men were being passed over the heads of the men in the line. We took about half a dozen wounded men – we didn't want to take them down to the cabin, it would be too painful for them to be moved, so we laid them out on top. Then the able-bodied soldiers in the line came on. We loaded up as many men as we could, and then we started off, heading back to the destroyers and other big ships.

Then the planes came. First it was Messerschmitts and Focke-Wulfs, machine-gunning. The able-bodied chaps laid their bodies over the wounded soldiers, to shield them from the fire. Shellfire was coming over, with the planes giving them guidance. Then there were the Stukas, the dive-bombers – you could see them coming at you, and the screech was awful. They dived down to about 500 feet and then let the bombs go, then they turned and machine-gunned at us on their way back. This went on all day and half the night.

We unloaded the soldiers on the big ships, then went back to the shore of Dunkirk for more men – back and forth, back and forth, all night and day. We kept going for three days and nights. Every now and then the cooks of the ships would appear with a huge corned beef sandwich and a mug of cocoa, and a can of fuel for the boat.

It was desperate. We saw people get hit and blown up, bits of bodies floating in the water. I was swiped in the face by an arm that had been blown off. All the time we had the fighters machine-gunning, and the shells coming at us, flying over constantly. I remember seeing some sailors in a rowing boat, like sitting ducks, and thought, "They've got no chance." Fortunately the sea was like a millpond. I've never seen it so calm – hardly a ripple, apart from the boats. But the pain and suffering is impossible to describe. The whole situation was so extreme, from the best in human nature to the absolute worst.

After one more trip, someone said, "That's enough – we're going home."

A lot of people landed at Dover, because that was nearest, but we were towed back to Chatham. From there, I went back to my unit, and at first they were angry with me. They thought I'd been absent without leave, as I'd only had a 48-hour pass. Fortunately

I'd asked an officer of the Navy to give me a letter explaining to my unit. So then they congratulated me instead, and I went back to my role as company runner.

The Blitz happened not long afterwards, in September 1940. I used a bike around the city, but during the Blitz it was useless because of all the rubble. Forty days or nights – hardly an hour when there wasn't a plane flying above us; maybe half an hour here, half an hour there when it was quiet, but the siren kept going on and on, bombs kept coming, and I had to carry on trying to do my job. We would lose contact with different groups and I would have to find them and set up communication again. Their bases became untenable and we had to find others. There were lots of nights without sleep – I remember one time I was up for five nights on the run, when we were based at White City. I remember coming back and being so exhausted that I slept for 36 hours straight through.

Then the Blitz stopped. It was hard to believe; it had become the natural thing. It was strange to find the city quiet.

Then our unit was given a different role, as guards of the British Home Force headquarters, which was stationed at Kneller Hall. I was put on a special duty job, guarding a private wall in the garden. At the time I didn't know what it was, but I found out later that they had brewed up some special gas in a bottle, and it had been broken in the corner. I was just supposed to stand there and make sure nobody approached it. Then the wind changed, and the next thing I knew I was in hospital. I'd been gassed, just like that.

After a few days in hospital, I was pretty much recovered and didn't seem to have any ill effects, so I was put back on duty, this time at the main gate. When you're a sentry you don't allow anyone, even the King himself, to come in without a proper pass. I was on duty at two o'clock in the morning and a car pulls up – it was the general himself, General Ironside. I knew him, but he didn't have a pass. I thought, "I've got a problem. If I let him in,

I'm in trouble." I called the guard commander – he came out and I whispered to him the problem, and he called the officer of the day. He knew that if he agreed to let the general in, he'd be in trouble too. So the officer of the day came, identified the general and he was allowed in. Only the officer had the authority to do it.

The following day at 10 o'clock in the morning I was posted to Chester for training – just like that, without any warning. I didn't mind though, because it was the first proper training I'd ever had. After the training in Chester, I was posted to Northern Ireland, to a regular unit, in the 2nd/8th battalion of the Middlesex Regiment. This was in early 1941. Whilst I was there I decided that since the war was obviously going to last for a long time, I should join the regular army, rather than just for the duration of the war. So I was transferred to the regular army. I thought, when this is over, there's going to be millions of men fighting over jobs – being a soldier suited me in some ways, so I thought I might make a career of it.

Things went along reasonably well in Northern Ireland, until the Americans came over and I had to do some manoeuvres with them, and had another accident. I was lying in a ditch with a couple of people, at the bend of a road, a place where you could set up an observation point. A truck came along with a heavy half-inch Browning machine gun on it, which hadn't been fastened down. As it came round the bend, it fell off the truck and hit me on the shoulder. My right arm was broken and bruised and I had slight concussion.

After six weeks in hospital, an army doctor examined me and they decided I was no more use to them. I was classed as unfit for duty, and discharged from the army on 22nd September 1942.

Chapter 5

Freedom Through Loving-Kindness

Fullness in Emptiness

You are not the conditions that make you do things. Gradually, you begin to see those as separate from you. You begin to lose the egoistic aspect of self and to realise the reality of a different kind of self which is unselfish and part of a whole. Consciousness can only communicate on one level – in feeling. It doesn't know anything else. It doesn't think; it has no organ for thinking. Consciousness is an aspect of the living condition itself, which all these things are wrapped around.

When you come to look, you have five senses: the eyes see, the ears hear, the nose smells, the mouth tastes and of course the whole body feels. Every part of it feels. The biggest sense organ is your skin. It's a fantastic organ, isn't it?

Let's think about sight. Does it see or does it feel? All colours produce a form of vibration which is picked up by the eye, which conveys the information back to the brain. So the eye in actual fact sense-feels as much as anything, in the same way as the skin, although you may not be aware of it. The same thing applies to smell – it's also feeling, although of a different kind. Hearing is also a vibratory feeling: taste is feeling. So consciousness only knows feeling.

Consciousness also knows the feelings you have for this or that. It knows the feeling you have between your inner feelings and your outer 'thinking' feelings, which are usually not together. But now and then they do come together.

Consciousness is what you should use for decisions, not the brain. The brain can be useful for discipline and concentration so that you can maintain an attitude over a period of time, where necessary. Then you can transfer into other areas and maintain a watchfulness in them, which might not be possible otherwise. When you learn to be constant in that, and patient, you can maintain the watchfulness in any position at any time, observing what is going, or what is *not* going on. The "not going on" is just as important as the "going on", so that we can learn to appreciate nothing as well as something.

We can appreciate emptiness as well as fullness. You wouldn't think emptiness could be appreciated would you? But it can be very important. Even in speech – if I used a language with multiple words with no gaps between, it would become incomprehensible. Between words there is a little gap, an emptiness, which brings understanding of my meaning. We don't realise how valuable emptiness is in our life of fullness. The gaps create understanding and provide a perspective. As a result, we should recognise the emptiness as much as the fullness.

When we move along the whole process meditatively, we arrive at a great emptiness, unbounded. But the emptiness is still full. Strange isn't it? The emptiness is full. Then we begin to see things differently. It makes sense and yet it is nonsense in the normal world. We know these things innately, and we have to open that door to innate knowing – which is, of course, the source of all life. When we know the nature of our life, we know the nature of everything.

We are experiencing it now this very moment. There is a body here, a body there, bodies all around the room, but somehow here we are bound together in this subtle feeling that we are all one. So the emptiness becomes full and there is only the one, with many manifestations within it. And it is very comfortable to recognise, isn't it? More comfortable than it was before. And is this not what we are really seeking in the world, to be at home within oneself and within our universe? That is what we have been looking for all the time, no matter what else we do. We tell ourselves, "If I do this I will be a bit happier." But *this* is what happiness really is, isn't it? It is that simple. We seek well-being in the wrong place, in the wrong form. It is not a worldly thing; it is an unworldly thing. The more unworldly we become, in this sense, the better off we become.

A Meditation

Do you have a meditation practice here?

This is one meditation I've developed, which I will guide you through:

Feel down here, a little bit above the navel – you'll find the right place. Centre yourself there, in feeling. Observe the breathing, in the sense of the expansion and contraction of the outer part of the body, as if it were a balloon. The body just breathes as it wants to, regardless of how you think it ought to breathe. Just observe this expansion and contraction for a few minutes...

You see it has a very calming effect. We are becoming quite peaceful... Just this gentle movement, this comfortable gentle movement... Again, look to the middle... Would you agree that it is peaceful? Absence of agitation, peacefulness... And within the peace would you say there is a kind of heartfelt warmth of feeling? It feels homely, as though you belong there... And as though it were a light...

Can you sense that warm peaceful feeling beginning to emanate beyond this balloon, through the rest of your body? All on its own, without any wilfulness, so that the physical body becomes the embodiment of this still warmth; homely feeling...

And again like a light, it begins to emanate even beyond the body... It reaches out all around in all directions... And begins to feel at home with all its surroundings, whether it be animate or inanimate... All of the same nature.

(Period of silence)

Now, gradually draw back into the very centre... Making sure it is still peaceful... and warm... Return to your normal consciousness...

Here, for a moment or two, we have been able to sharpen the consciousness to a degree, to its most subtle state, so it is not pointed in any way but spread, so it might detect the slightest movement, if movement were there...

You couldn't experience that peacefulness and warmth without a subtle form of feeling. It's not as coarse as the normal sense, and as it spreads further out, it begins to detect things of a deeper nature, which are always there, even though you never noticed them before. I won't tell you what they are; you'll find out for yourself.

It's almost as though consciousness is developing such gentle perception that you could compare it to a finger, soft and warm, touching a snowflake, sensing its nature, but so delicate that the flake doesn't melt. We should endeavour to develop that type of consciousness, with a similar expansive nature, in a peripheral sense. The whole 180 degrees, the whole 360 degrees, rather than just a limited point.

This is what gradually happens, as we become more familiar with this mode. Nothing will happen with meditation by itself. As you practise this gentleness of perception, of consciousness, you'll find that at any point in time in your daily life, you'll pick up on things that you never noticed before. This is where you begin to see the nature of things. When it happens in your daily living now – as opposed to in meditation – there is a reality, and we begin to see that what we perceive as normal is false. And this is how we free ourselves, by seeing the nature of things. It is not by any great effort, but by letting go that we achieve this.

Out of this, we begin to trust that deeper level of ourselves rather than the superficiality. In these moments, we become so expanded that we reach infinity, become boundless. This is the boundlessness of space. That is how big consciousness is, and we are only a small part of it, in our manifest form. But in reality we're part of that whole.

When that shift occurs, it's as if you are no longer contained in your body.

We move into a different dimension in which the body doesn't exist, because in this experience there is no body, is there? In that expansion or boundlessness, the body disappears. There is nothing below. It's almost like looking down a black hole; there's nothing there.

Generally speaking, this is the way to go. Sooner or later, as we become more familiar with this and as our consciousness becomes that little bit sharper, we begin to detect a different area altogether. We begin to detect certain entities of a different dimension, to sense presences around us, sometimes within us. This is quite normal, and quite proper at a certain point, as we begin to connect with the spiritual levels.

The angelic order – rather than people who have moved over – try to impress upon us, from within or without, their experience as though it is ours. But by the same token, in the angelic order they require some of our knowledge because they have never been born into this world. They take back some of our experience to help them, to find their way, even as we are trying to find our way. They pass us some of their experiences of a different dimension, so that gradually over a period of time, we begin to see that, yes, *this* is where I really belong, so that when death takes place there is no grasping at a body. You know that you're at home, so you don't have to grasp for birth.

We are coupled up with the angelic order unknowingly. I ask you to believe this; I'm preparing you for your own experience, so you won't think you're deluding yourself. There are one or two people here who have experienced some of these things already. There is a progression, and this involves a blowing out of the worldly conditions which hold you here. That doesn't mean to say it's a particular place at the end of the rainbow, a place that we were seeking. It's just a doorway through to something of a greater nature, which will still involve further progression.

Metta (Loving-Kindness)

The recognition of peace within is the doorway that opens up for metta – the warm, homely feeling of belonging. It goes out as an emanation. If you try to hold it, you lose it. It's because there is nobody there to hold it that it can expand. Through these practices we become the channel through which metta can enter from the spirit world into the physical world and through our bodies. It is the only time we can truly know it, in its passage through. That is why we cannot make it our own.

In that expanded area, I experience it as if it were a very gentle golden light that pervades the whole area.

All energies have a degree of light about them. This golden light is of course a manifestation of the metta aspect, the true love which is union, not separation. The purpose of repeatedly visiting there is to become more familiar with allowing an expansion of consciousness, openly and in every aspect of your life. Consciousness is the be-all and the end-all, so we should allow it to dissolve us into its very essence. Giving up self, dissolving into that greatness.

I do not believe in long meditation practices. Once you make contact and get the process going, a quarter of an hour or even 10 minutes is quite adequate. Do it seven times a day, until you have a continuum going all the time, rather than once a day. If there's a gap you lose the momentum, but if you keep it up, every couple of hours or so, there is a continuum. Switch it on, switch it off – learn to do that and you'll find you have a continual flow all the way through, which can even penetrate through to sleep as well. You could compare it to how a horse eats. Did you know a horse's stomach is only as big as a human being's? That's why it has to continually eat, all day long. It doesn't chew the cud, it goes straight through. In the same way, meditatively, here, there, there, there, throughout, we should maintain that quality.

This is one of the problems with early morning meditation in particular. The mind sometimes rejects it, because you're forcing it. In this way, the mind does it willingly all the time. It doesn't ever reject it, because it knows it will find peace in it.

I have had the experience a few times where I have felt my consciousness touch somebody else, experience somebody else. And they respond to it, without knowing.

Yes, it can happen. You can't make it happen, unless you just look and quietly absorb it. And you shouldn't do it for your own ends either; you should just allow it to happen, so that it's not you doing it anymore, it is happening through you. It's a spontaneous response, consciously, but not necessarily from your condition. Don't interfere with it, or try to take advantage of it. It is for the benefit of the whole, not yourself. In fact, meetings like this go far better when that happens! *(Laughs.)*

One of the things about the world that has always amazed me is that people believe that peace means to stop fighting. But it doesn't. Peace is freedom, not a cessation of hostilities. You need more than simply an absence of aggression. You need friendship, which means giving not taking. Receiving perhaps, but not taking. You need love, which comes from down *here*, not from the head. If everyone and everything could come down to this place of love, the world would be a totally different place. In fact, the world would not even exist anymore.

Freedom Through Metta

Sometimes you can have a deep sense of peace and well-being and you know that wherever you are in this world you can connect with it. And at the same time you send that ripple out. That same harmony can spread to all the people you come into contact with.

I agree with that up to a point but not wholly. You don't send the well-being out, you merely establish it within yourself. You become like the incandescent part of this bulb here; when it is lit, it just shines in all directions, it can't *not* do that. So if you have that as your stable base, the metta aspect, then that is all that is there, and that is all you can give, without any words or thought.

That's why it emanates throughout the whole. But you can't project it by thought. If you tried to, it would discriminate, whereas metta is for the whole world, not any particular individual. The sun shines on the righteous and the unrighteous; it makes no difference throughout the whole world. But you have to experience it, in order to radiate it. If you are angry, anger will be sent out. If you have kind thoughts but feel anger at the same time, it won't work. You can't pour milk out of a jug that contains water. If you have metta there, it will go out of you. If something else is there, thought won't change it.

This is where your practice – for example, chanting – will help. It will take you to that level, and if you can establish yourself there and use it as a base for all your activities, then metta will flow into everything you do. But that is quite a long way ahead. After all, the last sentence of the Metta Sutta says, "Those who are made perfect will not know rebirth." They are made perfect, with no aspect of desire or aversion. Only then does the state remain constant. But before then, you can keep touching into it, and come to know the benefits of it, and learn to avoid some of the things which hinder it. Hence the mindfulness aspect: to be aware of the things that might take you away.

This aspect is unqualified and therefore not conditioned in any way. So if a desire is eliminated, it won't be taken up by another one, or by aversion for that matter. You accept things the way they are. It's not easy, I grant you, but it can be achieved, if only little by little. And the more practice one does in this area, the more it will lead to greater areas of use. You might say it's like the thin end of a wedge, which goes further and further in until eventually there is nothing left.

Ego falls away; it weakens and weakens until eventually there is no desire for anything in particular, and whatever you look at is seen as empty, hollow, void, with no identity whatsoever, and of no value at all in the world. There is a greater fullness in a different area altogether; you are never wholly separate from anything.

It's an interesting thing when you come to pin it down to an everyday level. We're all so used to it: the 'I', 'You', duality. But is any sentient life – a person, animal, flower, whatever – completely separate from anything else? This 'I' – is it mine, or is it a combination of various factors coming from other people? If you meet someone who is irritated, how long before you take on the condition of being irritable? Is it yours, or theirs, or are you sharing it? And it's happening all the time, as you go through the day. When you meet other people, you begin to pick up their quality. It's like going to a foreign country – after a while, you begin to pick up their language.

So you can't say this is "me", because this "me" is a combination of many different factors. You can stabilise one area which is not disturbed by anything else, but even then that area still has contact with others, and even though other people's 'vibes' don't alter this, your 'vibes' alter that. So you will still be part of others but working in the opposite direction.

Sometimes when you meet someone, you have feelings for them – "I like this person", "I'm not too keen on that person." It's not intellect, it's feeling, isn't it? Even if they don't say anything you still pick up on their 'vibes'. How is it being done? Through an interchange of consciousness. So consciousness is a communicating factor between all things, that can carry whatever might befall.

Consciousness and the Unconditioned

To truly appreciate the results of the practice of the Buddha's teachings, you need to take on parts of the Christian aspect. The Buddha only dealt with the conditioned areas, how to eliminate them, so that there is a cessation of the conditions. Yet there is still the "Deathless". It's not the end, so where does it go now? There is still consciousness, and that has to live somewhere. It may still be where it appears, but in a different dimension. So you see there is a greater aspect. This is what the Buddha meant by Mind in the first place: "Mind precedes all things." In other words, it is unmanifest. Therefore consciousness is unmanifest. That's why it can operate within and without the body. It isn't contained, although it is attached by some means. We believe that we are separately conscious ourselves, but that is only a shadow of the real. Is it possible that consciousness is the be-all and end-all, and nothing to do with the conditioned world whatsoever?

Because of consciousness – the unborn, uncreated, unmanifest – we have the born, the created, the manifest, one to the other. This is a distinct area of oppositeness, so we assume the unborn, unmanifest, and so on, is an apparent emptiness which gives rise to a fullness and materialisation. In the unmanifest there is peace because there is no disturbance. But the moment you have manifestation, there is disturbance and chaos. In the unmanifest, there is a universal form of consciousness which is everything. In the manifest state, there is a constant aspect of separateness. We are so conditioned to the separateness that we cannot see the wholeness of the unmanifest.

This is consciousness. Without consciousness there is no life. If there were no consciousness, you wouldn't know life; you wouldn't know the world existed. There is a universal consciousness which is the whole universe – the spacious element, the emptiness apparent. Could there be a manifestation unless there was an emptiness, a space? Where would you put the manifestation? Is it possible that all matter that exists is an emanation from the emptiness, and does not disturb the emptiness in any way because it is made of the emptiness itself?

This is where the idea of God comes from. Suppose that what people normally think of as God is a vast consciousness. When Jesus said, "I and my Father are one," he was referring to that aspect of God. Not necessarily a physical father, but the consciousness which gave rise to the universe, and which is never separate from it.

Now when you reach the end of conditioning – when the grasping and the aversion have fallen away – this is what is left: consciousness is born into another area and begins to quietly assimilate its true nature, which has already been glimpsed to some degree in the physical sense.

All you really have to do is to examine these experiences as they arise, which means being very careful in the consciousness of observing. This is a very difficult thing because you can't control consciousness. You can use it, in the sense that you can know you're thinking thoughts you don't want to have and ask yourself, "Why can't I get rid of them?" Which part of you knows this? Which part of you is looking? If you were completely immersed in thinking you wouldn't know that you didn't want the thoughts.

It's almost as though there are two parts of you, one that is watching and one that is doing. The "doing" part of you is the thought mind, thinking up scenarios you find distasteful. The thought aspect is troubling, but the aspect that is observing is quite peaceful. It is consciousness in its own right. Is it possible that consciousness in its own purity can see these things? And I mean *purity*. Occasionally the purity is lost when we grasp at things of an impure nature. The important thing is to cast aside the impurities to gain access to the purity of consciousness.

All the time we are dealing with feelings. It's not physical; it's not manifest. A lot of these feelings come unbidden from somewhere unknown, because they are of a quality which is not of this world. Love and kindness in a world of chaos? It doesn't fit. It's an unworldly quality which we allow to come through. It is unconditioned. It only exists here for the moment that we experience it. Temporarily our grasping and aversion are dismissed, but when they emerge again we lose the quality. That is the true nature – the oneness, the wholeness, in the consciousness area. That truly is what we are.

Does that consciousness have inbuilt metta?

Its very nature is metta because it is total unity. We have separate bodies, but sometimes there is a rapport between us in which there is no separation. And that is not physical. When you practise meditation or chanting, there is a rapport which everybody shares. Is this not the one consciousness shared by all? This is something you already know and experience, but only temporarily. Suppose you could hold on to that? Well, that is the whole aim, to reach that point. That is why the conditions need to be allowed to fall away, in the Buddhist sense, so that this aim can be achieved.

Of the four noble truths, the one that matters most of all is the eightfold path, because this is the working aspect. The other truths are just theoretical information, but this is the practical path. Now if we deal with the aspect of *sila*, morality, then we begin to cool down our desires and aversions, and in doing so, we can reach into the metta. And when we reach into the metta, we find that it contains the whole eightfold path, all in one.

Identity

It is interesting that when somebody arrives here and understands the feeling, within a short space of time it's as if they've always been here.

They fit in very well don't they? Without any question of egotism, there's something very special about people who have moved themselves along. You can sense it and feel as one with them. You don't have to know who they are or what they are, but you can sense it: "Oh yes, there's one of us."

When I first came here you talked about putting all your awareness into your senses.

Is there any other experience you could have?

In the Western world we turn all that off. We're too busy rushing.

That's right, there isn't time to experience life. It's strange, isn't it? All animals use their senses to get around; we're the only ones that use our heads. And we are the ones in trouble *(laughs)*.

We have virtually destroyed our sense perceptions. A cat or a dog will sit there with one eye open observing what is going on, not particularly concerned about it. But we've lost the ability to do that – which means we have lost a lot. It takes a great effort to sit down and do nothing, or no thing. We've been taught to do everything the other way. There is more noise and disturbance around today than there ever was before.

The trouble with thinking is we have certain concepts associated with emotional states; and in thinking about those, we arouse the emotions and become lost in them. It's an interesting thing to examine how many different selves you have, associated with different feelings. And then, when you have a list of these different selves – and believe me it's a rapidly growing list – ask yourself: which is the real one?

You can't see yourself as others see you, and mostly you have the wrong idea anyway, because you assume others think as you do and usually they don't. It's important for us to feel that the world – at least the immediate world around us – approves of us. But when you understand that nobody sees the same way you do, then you realise that it doesn't really matter what other people think of you. You understand that everyone is operating from a selfish point of view; they're only concerned with themselves, or what you can offer them. They're not concerned about you. When you reach the point where you don't need or seek the approval of others, you can live comfortably. Then you can be free.

Never mind what other people may think – if you feel it is right for you, then it is right for you, and stay with it. If others don't like it, it is unfortunate. And as you learn more about others, you begin to give them more space, you begin to look at their nature, and compare your nature with that. This is how you come to learn about yourself. To that extent, the world becomes your teacher.

"Space" is actually quite a good description of the difference between being identified with a feeling and being less identified. In the less

identified state there is a space around the feeling. The feeling occurs within a spaciousness.

That's right. There is only that. And you begin to see as you go along how fleetingly small most of the incidents in life are – so small that they are almost non-existent. They are lost in space itself.

Chapter 6

Near-Death Experience

I went back to London and stayed with a friend. For a while I had a job at the Granada Tooting, a big theatre, looking after the heating and air conditioning. Then I got a call from the Ministry asking me to take up a course. I went to Hounslow and was trained as a maintenance electrician. We learned the very basics of electricity – lighting, wiring and power. After the course, I was posted to an airfield in Surrey that was still being built. I was amazed at how quickly they laid the runway – a 150-foot wide runway, two miles long, laid at a quarter of a mile a day, out of reinforced concrete.

There was one main runway and two subsidiary ones, in a triangular fashion, with a huge road all around them. Even whilst it was being built, once it was long enough, planes started using it. Our job was to maintain the electricity for the whole camp of about 10,000 people, to maintain the lighting of the camp and the airfield, and the perimeter lighting. There was a huge circle of lights, with a diameter of about 10 miles, all around the airfield. There was a series of poles with lights on the top, so that the aircraft would follow them around, and funnels to bring them on to the runway at night. They all had to be maintained. We also had a standby set for emergencies which consisted of a marine diesel engine, driving a huge dynamo generator. It had to be started by compressed air, so there was another motor to fill the compressed air tank, which also had to be maintained at all times, so it could start the engine. It was so huge that you could have stood up in one of the cylinders and got lost. Four cylinders, about 16 feet high.

Things went quite pleasantly at first. The runways were finished very quickly and aircraft were moved in. Mostly fighters to start with, Spitfires and Hurricanes. Then we had the medium bombers – the Mitchell bombers, Boeing planes, twin engines. We had to maintain the filters on the fuel tanks, maintain the pumps, aviation fuel, and the lighting in the bomb bays. We had to be very careful with these things.

We used to get the arrival of the big bombers. They would occasionally land after they had got shot up. I saw some fabulous things – I remember one Halifax bomber coming in, with half its wing shot away. There was one engine going on the outboard side, and half its tail shot away – and it landed on one wheel. How they managed it, how they steered it, I don't know. Things like that happened a lot. I admired these chaps immensely – for their courage.

Then the buzz bombs started. These were German motor propelled bombs, flying bombs coming over from France. Other people called them Doodlebugs. They just kept going until their fuel ran out, and then they came down. They were going about 450 miles an hour, so the Spitfires weren't fast enough to deal with them. They were a bit haphazard in their flight patterns, but a lot of them landed in London. Then the Typhoons came along, and Tempest machines, and they were fast enough to catch up to the buzz bombs. Twice I saw them fly alongside the Doodlebugs and tip their wings, to divert their course out into the sea. That took a lot of skill and courage.

After I'd been there for a year or two, I was instructed to go and check the power plinth, which was a little brick open-top building with an iron gate, where the power came in from the mains. It was transformed down from 33,000 volts into our circuit, then we transformed it down again. I went into this area to check it; it was probably going rusty and needed a bit of paint. But since it had been installed no one had ever bothered to look at it. Nobody knew that the insulation had broken down. As I went in, I gently brushed against a cable – as thick as my arm – and it hit me. I was literally thrown across the power line, where three cables fed into the transformer, to bring them to 250 volts.

I felt this mighty surge of power and my last thought was – quite casually, "Oh God, I've had it – this is the end." The next thing I knew I was out – not unconscious, but way out in space. Totally conscious but not conscious of me. No body, perfectly at peace. No sense of individuality. I was a thousand miles up in space, and I wasn't a person anymore. There was just a consciousness there, a glowing light. It was so serene, so peaceful.

I recognised that there was a huge amount of dark space, but there was light within it and I was that light. And then there was a knowing – not something that I was told, but something that I was just aware of. It became known that there was more which had to be done. My role wasn't finished. I was very content to be where I was, out there in space with that wonderful feeling of peace, but I realised that it was necessary to go back. Then I could see a tunnel, a tunnel through which birth could take place and I would return to the world again. But that would take too long, and what needed to be done was urgent. I didn't want to wait to be born again, so I looked back down at my body, laying across those three cables, and thought, "That's a mature body, it will save a lot of time if I can only get it going again."

It was the hardest thing I've ever done, to draw one single breath in my body, to allow the energy to start up again. My body was virtually paralysed, but I managed it. I found that my clothing was charred and the soles of my boots were scorched, but my body wasn't touched. Not a mark from 33,000 volts. I staggered out of the plinth, bumped into the wall behind, came out through the gate and lay on the grass outside, looking at this beautiful sky with the white cumulus clouds, thinking, "What the hell is going on?" And my boots were smouldering but I was perfectly alright, apart from being shocked.

It was another insight, another piece of awareness that there is more to life than appears on the surface. I didn't understand what it meant at the time, of course.

Then along came D-Day. We knew it was coming but we weren't ready for it. I was on night duty, in a little compound on the edge of the perimeter track where we had an office and workshop and bed; the place where we kept an eye on everything. At midnight a security clamp came down. And what I hadn't realised was that nobody had passes. Nobody had issued us with any; they assumed we didn't need them. So nobody was allowed in, including our relief. The sentries wouldn't let them in. It was another three days before that happened. So I was on my own for three days. And this was when things were really happening. The medium bombers were flying sorties back and forth all the time, day and night, to prepare for the ground troops. They were overloaded too, because it was only a short distance. They were supposed to have the capacity for four 500-pounders, but they put slings underneath the wings to put another couple on. They didn't need to take as much fuel, because it was such a short journey.

They were flying low, dumping down very precisely, trying to hold up the enemy so our army could get through. When flying back after being shot up, they would sometimes cause damage to the electrics on the runway. One time I was out there repairing the damage one plane had done on the side of the runway when another plane came in – he got rid of his wing bombs, but what I didn't know was that he had four bombs stuck inside, which he couldn't release. So as he hit the runway they all fell out and exploded. I was just a few yards away – four 500-pounders all blowing up at the same time. I was in a little manhole, working on the master circuit wires, which the other plane had damaged. The blast came over, whipped me out and I cracked my back on the iron rail. I thought I'd broken it, but I hadn't. It was extremely painful but I assumed it was just badly bruised. I didn't think any serious damage had been done, until later on in life. I've always had back problems ever since – badly damaged vertebrae. When I lie flat I get a lot of convulsive jerks.

During those three days and nights, I had to be constantly alert, without any sleep. The power would break down and I had to get it going again. I had to keep starting up the great engine. It all needed constant attention, and I had no relief. By the time somebody came in, I was exhausted. I virtually collapsed. I had another long sleep.

Chapter 7

Spirituality and Religion

The Traditional Path

Russel, do you have any observations about the Bhikkhus who visited last week? Do you think they enjoyed the meeting?

One of them originally came last year, and as a result of that he wanted to come back again to confirm what he saw, which he did. I know that because of the way he handled me afterwards. He hugged me. Bhikkhus don't do that!

In fact, last year, on his first visit, he actually knelt in front of me and put my hands upon his head. They were quite happy with what they found here. We did have a few words afterwards, which I'm not going to repeat, and found ourselves in total accord. A very good man, a very good man. He's the first person I've ever met with whom I've been able to communicate fully like that. When he came along last week I invited him to take over the meeting, and he said, "No, you do it," because he wanted to listen. I usually do that deliberately with other Bhikkhus, merely because I want them to see what happens here quite honestly, and to elicit their judgement. I did that with him the first time, but this time it was his decision.

He said that when he was a boy his mother was a devout Buddhist and taught him so much, and it was because of her that he eventually took the robe. After he came here the first time, one of the things he said to someone was, "Listening to Russel was like listening to my old mother."

He came along a traditional path, which works – of course it does. But you have to give yourself fully to it and take it past the teaching stages. It has to be taken in, to become inherent to you. I came to it in a totally different way without any knowledge of "Buddhism" whatsoever, and I saw the same thing.

Consequently we fit together like a hand in a glove.

They have the robe with their rules and strict formalities, but here it's all dropped, like a family – a family in the dhamma, you might say, family in spirit as much as physical. But of course I'm not really a Buddhist anyway! *(Laughs.)*

Whether you're a monk or not, whether you wear a robe or you don't, you can be equal. The point about it is, if you wear a robe you have rules which prevent a lot of things happening and can inhibit your relationship with other people, particularly women. As a layperson, occasionally you might hug somebody, and that hug can mean an awful lot to the person – not in a romantic or sexual sense, but in terms of compassion and understanding, if they are in difficulty. But as a Bhikkhu you can't do that. As a layperson you can do far more than you ever could in the robe, simply on the basis that you have a contact, a physical contact. Touch can mean an awful lot, even if it's just a hand on the shoulder. A Bhikkhu doesn't have that means of communication, only verbal.

We don't schedule Bhikkhus to come here – we don't invite them. They come because they want to, if they come at all. We've managed without Bhikkhus, and as far as I can see we've done a better job here without them than a lot of people do with them. We work differently, not through learning or teaching, but on a feeling basis, which is totally different. We work through presence rather than through words.

You don't need to listen to the words, you can sense-feel them, which is better than understanding. This is something I spoke about a few weeks ago, about learning to listen with the body rather than the head. It is wordless, based on experience rather than the intellect. It's surprising – you can understand the gist of things, without necessarily being able to put the meaning into words again.

My Teaching

We don't work with a sense of: "This is what the Buddha did, or what the Buddha said," or anything of that nature. We may refer to those things from time to time, or to other teachings for that matter, but words are meaningless as far as this goes. Here we operate through feeling, so that you can come to experience this from within yourself, gradually. As you cool down and relax, things begin to arise and you begin to *see*, even if it happens a day or two later. It is nothing to do with teaching.

I don't teach. You know that, don't you? That is why we can have such diverse aspects of conversation from time to time, because it all leads to a degree of rapport, which is the most important thing. Out of that rapport *you* become at one with yourself, and in that oneness of self, things begin to happen. But other groups don't operate this way, to my knowledge. They're usually based on intellect, intellect, intellect. Here you become more natural to yourself, which is the way it should be, because you are the source of anything you need to know, not me. That is the way you come to knowledge, by gently accepting. So it is a tuning-in process more than anything else.

Have you ever written anything?

I tend to respond to the situation at a particular moment, to respond to people individually, even though there may be a group. There is no set formula, no lectures or sense of learning. More often than not the teaching will direct itself to an individual and yet that of itself is sufficient for everybody else at the same time. To me, the impression counts far more than the words. One isn't concerned with being a teacher at all, only with responding to the needs of a person at a particular point in time. I don't do anything – I merely open a channel for something to operate through me. It's not me as an individual, but that which comes from the greater areas. I don't know what's going to come through, and I don't decide what is right. I've learned to trust it all so much that it just works.

If it was written down, a person would only read it according to their understanding, not as it was originally meant. They would read it in terms of content rather than its *nature*, which is what people respond to. Sometimes one will say black is white to one person, and white is black to another. But it's the same message *(laughs)*. People's understanding works in different ways, from different angles, and you have to meet each of those. It doesn't really matter if it's contradictory, provided the truth lies within it and the listener picks up their truth out of it, even though it might be the wrong way round. It's the rightness that matters, not the content.

Think of a mountain with different paths up to the top. If you come up on one side, and another person comes up the other, you can't see one another because you can't see over the peak. Now suppose you were able to communicate with one another – you would say, "I can see this." "This is what I can see." You see different things. You may be both 100 feet up, but the experience is totally different, from one side to the other. You can't communicate without confusion until you reach the top. And then you realise: "Ah, both paths lead to the peak."

This is one of the difficulties that occur when people start to meditate. Someone says, "I had such an experience," and another person thinks, "I ought to have had that experience too." No. Your way is different, therefore your experience will be different. It is only later, when you're more deeply involved, that you begin to realise it's the same thing in essence. It's like seeing the front of the house and the back of the house, and describing them differently. It seems like a different place, but it's just a different way of looking at the same thing. Comparing notes too early can be confusing. Later, of course, once understanding has developed, then comparing notes can be helpful.

Beyond the Buddha

I think you will agree that most people who come here – once they've settled into the atmosphere – feel as if they've been here all their lives. And it's true – in spirit, you have been here all your lives. The original members of this society opened a keyhole into the spiritual world, and that is what this house represents. In modern terms, you might call it a wormhole into another dimension. And spiritually, all of you are connected to that, even if you don't know it. So what happens here isn't necessarily due to me, but due to what is coming through me, from this place. I can't take any credit for anything. What comes out is not mine.

This is what makes this place unique. It is not other than what the Buddha knew, although it is not what he taught. The Buddha was a very wise man, a brilliant man, to be able to identify, assess and describe all those aspects of a person that bring suffering, and to show them how to become free of them and gain clarity of mind. But he didn't go beyond that. He only spoke of the Deathless; he never mentioned any spiritual worlds as such. He didn't speak of communication with other entities, as far as we know.

But this is what we deal with here. The mind opens up; we begin to see that there are other dimensions which may not be immediately obvious. We move into what you might call the Christ area – not Jesus, but the Christ spirit, which was the first great spirit that came into being. The Christ spirit is the God spirit, you might say, although not in the sense of a primary God. It is a vast area of consciousness, and Christ was the first manifestation out of it. Therefore he is the doorway; the beginning of manifestation.

We are all aware of that which is manifest, but we're not aware of the process of becoming. That is why we have to go back to the stillness, the emptiness. As we come out of it again, we can see how it builds up into worlds, and that shows us how to go back to where we belong, as spirit entities rather than physical ones.

Buddha Dhamma and Christianity

The Dhammas recognise the causes of things, whereas dhamma suggests the doing of them, without necessarily recognising any causes at all – "I'm hungry, so I'll eat." On the other hand, the Buddha dhamma is the recognising of the basic processes of your mind – how you attach to things or let them go, how you become averse to things, and how you begin to form the conceptual area of the mind whereby you judge things as right or wrong, good or bad. This is Buddha dhamma. But to 'do', unknowingly, is plain dhamma. Dhamma means doing, whereas Buddha dhamma is recognition of the doing.

You can say two things about this: there is Buddhism as a belief system and there is the way of the Buddha, which is a recognition system. The latter is totally different and doesn't require any book learning at all. When you have book learning, a belief system arises, and at very best, this will only help to create an even state of mind for a short period of time. This is *samatha*, which you have to keep renewing because it is conditioned, as opposed to *vipassana*, which leads to the opening of the mind to see things clearly, and does not require any historic or intellectual material at all.

This is the difference between Buddhism and the way of the Buddha: the latter is not learning but being. Christianity is a belief system too, until you reach the point of recognising yourself as one with God. But Christianity itself does not recognise the oneness; it is always separate, dualistic, in contrast to the words, "I and my Father are one." According to the Bible, Jesus "sits at the right hand side of God the Father Almighty" – separate, not as one at all. They're talking about Jesus as a man and God as a spirit; they are separate and always will be. They're not talking of the Christ spirit that entered into Jesus, which was still the Father. It is the Christ that matters, not Jesus.

If there is oneness, there is the possibility that your congregation may acquire oneness without you being an intermediary.

The church doesn't want that because it means they would lose power. That's why they killed the Gnostics and Cathars. There were a few partly enlightened people who saw things differently and formed sects – the Quakers, the Methodists, and others from Germany, Austria and France.

The Orthodox Church in Greece and Russia is a different matter altogether. The Roman church is corrupt; the Eastern Church is the true one, and has remained true right from the beginning. A number of people have found that once their mind has become clearer and emptier through following Buddhism, they see Christianity differently and as they examine it again it becomes very real. Buddhism can be a way into Christianity. Buddhism deals with the physical side of life, and once you've begun to see things more clearly, you can recognise the spiritual side of life and follow that. At that point, it's not a belief anymore, but a way of being.

Spirituality and Religion

Occasionally one meets religious people who have a genuine spiritual quality.

Oh yes, but they are few and far between. Where there is spirituality there is freedom, but religion is rigid. To be spiritual you have to step aside from the belief and go more into knowing, which gives you a greater freedom, including the freedom to question. Unless you question you're not going to get past the beliefs.

I am not saying religion is not a useful thing. It can provide a form of morality, which is good for the community. But it can easily become heavy and rigid, leading to the condemnation of others, which is not a healthy thing. If taken in a moderate way, most religions are benign and helpful. It's only when they get uptight that things go wrong. When that rigidity appears, it's almost as if the Satanic element is coming in.

Religion really needs to be looked at from a different angle.

Even Buddhism is often taught in the wrong way, from the intellect rather than the heart. If you are brought up to feel it as much as think it, then you're in a better situation, because you're experiencing the very qualities you are trying to express. When you sense-feel it, it's completely different from just going along to services and rituals, without any great meaning.

Can that be taught, do you think?

To a degree, yes. It requires a particular quality of person who can instruct in these matters. It has to be somebody with real heart and feeling and a concern for others. Then you can begin to open up people in that way. Young people in particular – children can be brought up in a very loving and kindly atmosphere, realising that love can be a part of religion, and that even the words can bring comfort within. Not everyone would pick this up, but some would. It has to be done in such a way that it creates interest in the person who is learning, to make them ready to absorb.

After all, religions are supposed to bring about a brother or sisterhood amongst people, and you can only do that by accepting them as part of a family, rather than 'another person'. When we have that kind of atmosphere, people begin to sense-feel and hear a path of belonging. They feel less individual, a part of a group, so that the idea of a separate ego diminishes to a greater extent; there is more outflow taking over. A sharing of one's life with others. A realisation that we are not separate from others.

Everybody needs to be looked at in the same light. What light? In the light of the fact that they are all pilgrims on the same path. Their path may be different, it's true, but it's the same thing ultimately. Some may be totally ignorant of the fact they are on the path, others may be well aware of it. This applies to all sentient life – even animals can eventually rise into the human and are therefore still on a path. As the Buddha said, "There are but few with little dust in their eye that are able to see the truth."

Even in human beings there seems to be such a massive range of different levels. Some human beings are very highly developed...

Yes, but it doesn't mean you should respect someone who is 'up there' more than you would someone 'down there'. The latter person still has a long way to go, whereas the other has already travelled. The person 'down there' perhaps needs a little bit of a help or a pull up *(laughs)*. Developed people are raised up and put on a pedestal, but they shouldn't be. You should keep them down here to work, on the same level as you. Then you can communicate. If they're too high up, you can't reach them. People tend to look up to people at a higher status, but it is only another journey. Keep it down here.

Chapter 8

Wandering and Transformation

During all those years, especially as a teenager, I was full of anger. I was angry with myself because of my ignorance. I was aware of suffering in the world, and I knew there was some meaning behind it, but I couldn't get close to understanding it, and so it filled me with frustration. And my anger manifested itself as aggression. I had no time for other people; no patience or empathy. Other people irritated me, and if they crossed me, they were in trouble. To make things worse, I was very strong too, with a hair trigger temper. A dangerous combination. When I was working on the farms, I could pick up a sack of potatoes in each hand, a hundredweight, and just throw them. Plus, I had no fear. I was never afraid of anything. I had a lot of fights and I could easily have killed someone. The anger burned inside me for a long time.

Back when I was still in the army, I was escorting someone down to Shepton Mallet and had to go through Waterloo Station. As I walked along, who should I meet but my own brother. He was on his way home, on survivors' leave after his boat had sunk. It was the first time I'd seen him since our mother died. Through him I found out where my sister Betty was. When I had the opportunity to go and see her, I discovered that she'd had a rough time of it too, working as a skivvy for our aunt. It was because of the aunt's jealousy of my mother – because she'd originally thought Dad was going to marry her, and he'd chosen Mum instead. So when my sister went to live with her after my mum's death, she'd taken it out on her.

When I visited, I found that this aunt was wearing my mother's wedding ring. She had taken it all those years ago, when they ransacked the house after she died. "You shouldn't be wearing that," I said to her. "Why didn't you give it to Betty?"

"No," she snapped back. "She was my sister, so it should be mine."

"But Betty was her daughter."

"She's not getting it."

"What makes you so sure?"

I had some bullets in my pocket. I was so angry that I pulled one out and held it up. "See this bullet – it's got your name on it. If Betty hasn't got the ring by the end of the week, you're getting it."

It was cold anger. And I would have done it; they could tell by my rage that I would have. So when I went back on Saturday to check, Betty was wearing the ring.

I was a wreck at the end of the war, emotionally a mess, weary and fed up.

I'd been battered around so much that I felt broken down. When you added all the experiences together, from the beginning to the end of the war – plus all of the suffering I'd experienced earlier in my life – there wasn't going to be a quick recovery from all that. I felt like I'd had enough. All I wanted was to get away from myself.

After D-Day I resigned from my position at the airfield straight away. I took a job as a handyman at a school for evacuated kids, out in the country. I'd made plans with a colleague at the airfield to start up an electrical business. That was the plan. At the end of the war, there were so many repairs which needed doing, so much electrical work, that we thought there was an opportunity there. But as we were about to do this, I had a realisation.

It was a Sunday, I remember. I felt as though I needed to think about what was happening in my life. I asked myself: "What do you really want in life?" I was only in my early 20s but I'd been through so much misery. The only part that had been reasonably happy was the early part of my childhood. Since then there had been nothing but horror. So I asked myself, "What do I really want out of life?" And I answered myself: "I want to be happy." And I realised that if I followed this path – starting up this business – it wouldn't make me happy.

There were several different paths I could have taken but a part of me said, "No" to every one. Something inside told me, "All of those aren't going to take me where I'm supposed to be going, they're going to take me further away." I was in a dilemma. I couldn't go on as I was.

The only thing left was to walk away – literally – and hope that something would show me where I was supposed to be going. So I left, with just a few shillings in my pocket. It was the summer of 1945. I started walking, and carried on, walking and walking. I lost track of time. It could have been weeks or months. I slept under haystacks and hedges, washed clothes in little brooks and laid them out in grass for the sun to dry. Every now and then I mended an old fence for a sandwich and a cup of tea. I remember pulling a swede out of the ground and chewing it, because I was so hungry. But most of all I remember the sunshine – the sun always seemed to be shining.

One day I was walking across the moors, and I came across a showman with a broken-down bus. He was sitting on the step of the bus with a pot of tea in his hand. I came up to him – I must have looked in a desperate state. He looked up and said, "You look like you could do with one of these." He made me a pot of tea, and I sat down with him. He asked me, "When did you last eat?"

"I don't know – a couple of days ago, I think."

He gave me a meal, then after we'd chatted for a while, he asked, "Do you want a job?"

"Yes, I'll do anything. Tell me what you want me to do and I'll do it."

"Do you know anything about horses?"

"No – all I know is you feed them in one end, and they crap

out of the other."

"Well it doesn't really matter – if you can get to Newquay by 7 in the morning, there's a job for you there, looking after horses."

He gave me half a crown, and sent me on my way. Newquay was about 70 miles away – how I managed to get there I don't know. I left at five o'clock that evening and arrived there dead on seven in the morning, just as they were beginning to pull out, a small circus with a few trucks and horses following behind. I handed over a note that the man with the broken-down bus had given me. They stuck me on a horse, gave me another one to lead, and I followed them to the next site. We set up the show there, then sat down and had breakfast.

The show was run by Tommy Reany, a fairground man, who thought he'd try his hand at a small circus, as a trial, to see how it worked. He'd borrowed these horses, which had already been trained, and there were a few lads and girls, acrobats, wire-walkers, clowns. He gave me a pound a week, and I had food and somewhere to sleep.

I stayed with them for the whole season, then Tommy Reany arranged another job for me, on the boards in Chesterfield Theatre. This was a show with three lions, about 10 horses, a mule and two little ponies. I dressed the horses for the show, led them into the ring, then at the end of the show I worked with a clown called Andy, putting waterproof blankets on the horses and taking them down to the stables, a couple of miles away. We would jump on one horse and string up the others, so there was a long line of them following behind us, back to the stables. That was where I slept too, in a camp bed.

I began to groom, feed and water the horses, and learned how to use the different harnesses. We toured a few theatres, then headed down south for the winter. There was an old Air Force station in Braintree, Essex, and Chipperfield's was wintering there with their show. We were in the next hangar along.

Chipperfield's was buying bigger new tents, and we borrowed their old ones. We had to create a circus from scratch, so as well as looking after the animals, I helped build up the ring fence, and the seating, and painted the trucks. It was a tough winter, very hard work. I grew to love the animals. I felt a strong connection with them. It was impossible not to, living with them 24 hours a day. I was determined that I was going to understand them wholly, for what they were, and realised that the only way to do that was through observing them. I knew I wasn't going to get the knowledge from reading books. So I set my mind to watching and observing every detail, every moment of the day, for days on end.

After about three months, as I became more concentrated on the horses, I noticed that I wasn't thinking anymore. My mind had gone quiet. I realised that knowing and thinking are two different things, and that you could know without thinking. I wasn't forming opinions or jumping to conclusions anymore. I began to do things spontaneously, to live in the moment. I had a strong feeling that I was finally going in the right direction, that this was my path, and I should keep going with this, carry on observing the animals so intently.

It wasn't till much later that I realised that the exercise I'd given myself was mindfulness meditation. In effect, I was meditating about 20 hours a day, 7 days a week for three years, completely absorbed in caring for the horses. It was a life of continual service, with no thought for myself.

Then it happened. I woke up one morning and looked across at the horses, watching the steam rise out of their nostrils the way it does on a cold morning. The next thing I knew I wasn't just observing the horse, from the outside. I *was* the horse. I was looking inside it. I was it. I could look through its eyes and its mind. I was aware of its true nature. I was aware that all things are one. There was a sense of profound peace within me.

It was a revelation. I looked at another horse, and another, and I was inside them as well. I looked at one of the dogs, and saw it in its true nature too. I saw everything in its true nature. I went outside to look at the lions and it was the same with them – looking from the inside out, not the outside in. We were all the same nature, all arising from the same source. My own nature was just as theirs was, in a different form, with one consciousness linking us all together. They were only separate in terms of form and structure. It was the same essence, the same emptiness, in all of them – in all of us. I went outside to look at the trees, and they were the same nature. Then I looked at my own body, and inside myself, and there was nobody there. My normal sense of self had disappeared.

At that moment there was no more anger, no frustration, just a sense of peace. There was no desire, no aversion; everything was as it should be.

Chapter 9

The Ego

Karma

Do you think the floods in Pakistan at the moment are connected to karma?

Natural disasters like earthquakes and floods are purely random. They're nothing to do with karma whatsoever. If you are in the place where one occurs, the only karmic aspect might be whether you accept the event, or find it fearful and become frightened. But they have nothing to do with the karmic aspect itself. Karma is individual, within you. It's nothing to do with outside events whatsoever, other than it may react to them. That's all.

People can be lucky, or unlucky, in where they are born, in different countries.

I wouldn't say that necessarily. Generally speaking, you are born in the place and within the social circumstances that may be necessary for your development. Whether or not you develop at all makes no difference to that. You can take advantage and use it to help you work your way up; but if you don't, you remain at that level.

One aspect of karma I would like to emphasise though – which is very rarely mentioned – is how it can be influenced by other people. If you're aware of karma you need to take a little care, because it's so easy for your state of mind to change in the presence of others. It's so easy to be influenced into an unpleasant state of mind, in which you do things from an unpleasant motivation. Changing your state of mind means changing your karma.

This is where the metta principle is so important. If you can establish yourself in the feeling and experience of metta, you can withstand the negative influence. Nothing can disturb you; the influence will just bounce off. And your presence will help to cool other people around you, because of that peaceful aspect. If you can retain that peace, then your karma will always be healthy, whatever you do, and you will pass a little of that on to whoever you meet, so that their karma will be better. By the same token, if you feel uneasy, that will be passed on to other people, and their karma will be worse. So if you can stabilise your own state, you can do an awful lot of good for other people's karma by helping them to cool down and develop metta. As a result, over a period of time they will be able to lift themselves up to see things a little more clearly.

So be aware of your inner state and keep it as peaceful as you can for the benefit of those around you. And not only that, it makes it much more peaceful for you yourself, through people's response to you. It's like the ripples of a pond: you throw a stone in there and it ripples out, and you never know how far the effect will spread, either negative or positive. But it's up to you and me to be as positive as we can to help the people around us, many of whom are quite frankly in a hopeless condition. They have a karmic cycle, whether they know it or not.

Karmic Development Through a Clear Mind

From that we turn to something of a different nature, again related to the karmic cycle. This is something I think you will be quite happy about: people may tell you that you have to have everything worked out before you become enlightened, but it's not true.

What we find is that, as you open up your conscious awareness and live more carefully, little bits drop off the karmic wheel. And as the bits drop off, your mind becomes even clearer. So when you're about halfway through the wheel, roughly, your mind may be so clear that you're able to see the whole thing as delusion, in which case the second half of the wheel doesn't exist anymore. That's a big help – half your battle gone.

You don't keep making karma, endlessly. All you do is renew the old, which makes you think that you're making more. But you're not. When the old karma is triggered and crops up again, if you can recognise it as it arises and let it go, it drops off and there's another bit gone. If you don't recognise it, it will take hold again, and renew itself. This is where you think you are making more karma, although you're only giving rebirth to the old. So you only have a molehill, which never becomes a mountain. It is only an illusion that karma seems to be increasing. So, again, this cuts down the battle.

Think about it – all of you are old enough now to be aware that certain things keep cropping up every so often, things of a very similar nature. This is your mark of how your cycle is turning. This is simple, but it makes a big difference.

Ignorance and the Nature of Happiness

One of the most positive approaches to life is to know what not to do, as much as what to do. It is a very good safety factor. You should observe the suffering of the world closely, but make sure you don't get contaminated by it. Notice it, be aware that it's there, but make sure you don't get wet with it.

The degree of ignorance in the world is incredible, in the sense that people keep pursuing things that bring them more unhappiness, rather than pursuing those which can bring contentedness. And the contentedness is always there, if we look underneath the things we want, or don't want. We are attached to things we like, or even to things we don't like, and if we let them both go we'll find we are already content. But we are not prepared to do that. It doesn't take any effort at all just to be content. Yet we strive and strive and strive to make ourselves unhappy, on the pretence that we are going to be happy *(laughs)*.

It's a question of not realising the true nature of things. When you look at the depth of this ignorance, you realise what a brilliant man the Buddha was, to understand the importance of these three aspects: greed, hatred and delusion. In other words, grasping, aversion and ignorance – including ignorance of the fact that one of the other two drives us all the time, if not both. And ignorance of the fact that they are not ours anyway; we just identity with them.

Curious isn't it? We're deluded into believing that we are not happy and that therefore we must make ourselves happy. But we find spontaneity, and with no self-effort, we realise that we were already there. We've been trained, and have trained ourselves for so long, to chase after the myth – so we continue to chase, even though the myth is not there. The things we chase after may give us a little elation here and there, but that will die and switch to the opposite. When we stop chasing we realise that we already had contentment. We were running away from it, not towards it. Happiness is already here, just waiting for you, to just *be* there. It does not require any effort at all. All it requires is letting go.

Without a taste of that 'something' it is a big leap in the dark to abandon these things.

Yes it is. You're so accustomed to the unpleasantness that you don't trust the pleasantness. It has reached the point where many people nowadays find it very difficult to just stop and slow down enough to experience the qualities of stillness. They can't bear it, can't abide the thought of being still and quiet. It's strange when you think about it – it's not a question of looking for it in other people. You had it yourself at one point, and it was only by chance that you lost it. You've often had little glimpses but have ignored them and passed on, not realising they were opportunities to follow, offering a way out. Then at some point maybe there was a wider gap, and you realised there was something there, and so followed it.

You recommend metta, introducing a kindly attitude.

Yes I do, but it's strange to use the word 'introduce' when this is your basic nature. Imagine you're walking along and you see a plant coming up through the ground, or a kitten, or a dog, whatever it may be – and your heart opens out. Metta is already there, spontaneously, without a single thought taking place. So why do we have to seek it?

You Are Not the Body

How do we know we are separate from thinking, and from the physical? By our own observation. You might think, "I know I am me. I am me, I am in control of what I do and what I think." Suppose I tell you that you are not. Would you believe that?

If you are in control, why do you think thoughts you don't want to think? How do you know you are thinking thoughts you don't want to think? Is there something separate which watches thinking going on? If you are watching, who is doing the thinking? If you are thinking, who is doing the watching?

So somewhere we have to make a separation. If thinking is a process of the brain, which is part of the body, it is merely a process going on within the physical structure. Therefore I am the watcher. I am the consciousness that sees the process. Therefore I am not the body. Is that possible? Consciousness is spirit, not physical. If it were otherwise, the body would know all of this without organs of consciousness.

The body is not all that important, apart from as a vehicle. It is the base in which our conscious perceptors reside – sight, sound, taste, touch, smell. But take those away and who are you? There is nothing. We are the consciousness that works through the body, although it is not of the body. As we move along quietly, we begin to see that we are not confined to the body. And when it passes, the body leaves us free, at least momentarily, to move into a different area, until we find another body – unless of course we reach a point of realisation of our own nature to the extent that we don't need another body.

All physical things are constructs out of that consciousness, necessary and useful because there is duality rather than unity, and you can learn far more quickly from duality than you can through a unity process. I would maintain that these animal bodies have no particular intelligence of their own – consciousness is the intelligence itself. And since consciousness was there before the body, the body does not create consciousness, but vice versa.

Shut your eyes and, without thinking, tell me what shape is your body?

Setting aside all concepts and ideas, do you know the shape of your body? All you are aware of is a spherical area, is that true? All we have is awareness. So that is you, not the body.

The Observing Self

Where does instinct come from?

Instincts are direct recognitions of consciousness itself rather than the body. It's not easy to understand that consciousness and the thought activities – or physical activities – are not the same. But with a little care and attention – particularly when you find yourself thinking thoughts that you wish you didn't have and which you can't get rid of – you realise that it's as though there are two of you. There is the chaotic thinking mind and the part of you which is observing that chaotic mind and its thought-contents. Within the thought-mind itself there is an emotional attachment which gives it a strength and a flavour, whereas the consciousness aspect is observing in a detached way, almost as if it's saying, "What's this all about? We don't really need this."

While the nature of the thought aspect is chaotic – particular with the addition of emotion – the nature of the observing aspect is quite peaceful, completely free of disturbance. These are two direct opposites, and which one are you? Are you the observer, or are you the doer? If you are the doer you lose the observing aspect of consciousness, but if you accept that you are the watcher instead, then you begin to see that the doer or thinker is not 'you', but a process going on, over which you have no control.

Once you see this, ego begins to diminish. We gradually begin to realise that consciousness is what I truly am – not this chaotic condition whereby any external thing can start a whole chain of thought (with accompanying emotions), because it has been conditioned to respond in that way. And it's nothing to do with you at all. When you can remain with the conscious observer, gradually the clockwork begins to slow down and doesn't get wound up again *(laughs)*. And so we begin to get free of the chaotic condition, and as it slows down we can see it more clearly and realise that it's not the way for us to go. So we just leave it be and let it die. We become clear of it by being purely conscious, and realise that the consciousness is a flow taking place from somewhere other than oneself. It is something which is flowing through – and eventually you realise that it's flowing from the universal. I and my father are one. I am part of that; it is not other than me. A strange identity which is not a me anymore *(laughs)*. A joke, isn't it?

As one begins to appreciate it for what it truly is and to see the benefits that have already arisen – in the sense that one is already living more peacefully within oneself and with those around us – then we open ourselves up more to this flow, until we become a whole clear channel. So the greater aspects of the greater consciousness operate through this minor one here, until the two become as one.

Beyond Duality

Here we have reached the culmination of the Buddha's teaching. We have dispensed with the conditions that hold us in thrall to the physical world. We are dealing with a phenomenon we have always been aware of but didn't realise was not part of the physical world – in other words, feelings. Feelings of our relationship with any person, or animal and plant – they are very subtle, precise, and don't require understanding. In fact, there are some feelings which you can't understand. This is spirit.

Having reached this culmination point by disposing of most of these problems, we are beginning to see these feeling areas, and we come to discover the nature of consciousness, which we can only know by experience. Here we become aware of the true nature of self, where there is no egoistic self.

In fact this is where reversal takes place. All aspects of self or ego are separate, dualistic. They are always to the benefit of me. *This* is the prime thing to be looked after, not other people. But when we reach the point of the cessation of these conditions and meet the true nature of the consciousness, the opposite process occurs – nurturing, giving out, giving. And in this we lose duality, because in the giving we become *that*. And it is the only time we are ever really happy. There is nobody there to give; it's just a flow. In religious terms, God is love. Consciousness is love in its nurturing sense. The basic nature of all this is to nurture.

It's so natural and simple – that's the joke of it. But it is not easy to achieve. In fact I will state the opposite here: to attain this realisation, to attain freedom, is the most difficult thing that anybody ever attempted in the whole world. It is relatively easy to put an argument across and make somebody believe it. But to release ourselves from all these arguments is the most difficult thing in the world.

To have a mind without thought; to know without thought. The Buddha teaches us to be still, to be silent. Stillness means no thought. But to be wholly conscious of the stillness and the apparent emptiness, which is vast – that is very difficult. This is the Biblical saying, "Seek ye the peace which lies beyond understanding." Beyond understanding – you can't think your way to it, only practise the experiencing of it. It is already there.

It must be realised that you can't experience spirituality in thought alone. It has to be in experience. Think about it all you like – it won't change a thing. But when you begin to realise through feeling, everything will change. Thought is neither honest nor constructive. It's destructive because it takes you away from the real.

I think one of the best pieces of advice you gave in the early days, Russel, was when you said that when you open a door, treat the handle as if it's an eggshell, and do it gently. I have always remembered that and applied it.

It is practice which reflects back on you. The world is a mirror. Everything manifest is a mirror. Whatever quality you put out will be reflected back to you. This is what mindfulness is all about: to be well aware of the condition in here, and make sure that what you give out is of the same nature. If you want to live peacefully, give peace. If you want chaos, put chaos out there and you'll soon get it back *(laughs)*.

If you are wise, you learn to be very, very gentle in almost everything you do. Then you get that subtlety of feeling, and it is the subtlety that matters most. It means slowing down somewhat. Not allowing immediate response. Wait. Be gentle. Does it really need a response? If it does, take it gently. There's no need to be tough. And also, whatever you do, give it your full, undivided attention.

Often you come to know rather than understand. Thought has its place; nobody is denying this. But it must not be allowed to overtake everything else. There are times when we need to think about things, but if those times are not present, we don't have to think. If you stop thinking about them, they will still be there when you need them. But in between thoughts, you can learn to experience what is there. That is where living takes place. In thought there is no living, only delusion.

Giving Full Attention to Household Tasks

If you give your whole attention, your wholehearted attention, to any person, if only momentarily, you'll see how they respond and blossom. They will feel, "I am recognised, I am a somebody." But if you give half-hearted attention, whilst you're thinking of something else, they'll feel, "I'm not here; I am not being recognised." People need that recognition.

The same applies to household tasks: dusting, polishing, washing the floor, washing the dishes, and so on. Give them your full attention, don't think of other things. The now is all there is, so learn to live in it. And surprise, surprise, when you do, all fear disappears. The alternative is to live in fear all the time, through being concerned about what might happen next. But if you are only in the now there is no next moment. Strangely, you can move through time with this attitude – with full attention here, there, there, there, there – but it's all one continuous moment. There is no tomorrow.

Am I really saying that you should give your whole attention – with a loving aspect – to a piece of crockery? Yes. As if it were a living creature. In the moment of doing, the object reflects your love back to you by virtue of its mirror action. Try it and see – this will produce a wonderful karma. Whenever you come to do these tasks, be it washing the dishes or washing your socks or stockings, whatever, do them with your whole attention just for those moments; gently, carefully, as if you're dealing with a living creature. Observe how you feel and you'll find it's really worthwhile. A lot of extraneous thoughts disappear, things that would otherwise worry you, so that you have a contented mind which you carry with you to the next activity. You begin the new task contented, free from agitation, and see things more clearly, so you're able to deal with every situation better. You don't have to do anything special, just the things you normally do, but with your full attention.

You might forget to do it of course – if so, try again and watch how the process works. Once you realise how it works, and once you experience its benefits, you'll continue to do it. It'll enter into different parts of your life more and more and you will be much more content. This is the way of the spirit. Your spirit is being indulged and shared within the world, with inanimate objects as well as animate. You'll become much more friendly to other people and they will begin to respond, after a period of time, if not immediately. Some people take longer than others. I remember, from my own experience, one particular person whose mind took me two years to change. But that was an exception.

Generally, this is the way we can begin to change ourselves, in little everyday things that don't require a great deal of effort at all. Where possible, we should give ourselves a bit of time and sit down for 10 minutes, be still, quiet, and allow things to subside and to feel deep within ourselves the still peacefulness from which the nurturing arises. Just like that.

There's a bit of a joke here: it's been said that Buddhist monks spend their time contemplating their navels. Actually, there is a lot to be said for that, because that's where that still small space is, deep within the body. If you allow your consciousness to drop down into that area and be more peaceful and expansive in consciousness, you find it is very warm and comforting and that it takes you away from the 'thinking box' for a while.

So in that way you can learn to be still. You don't have to try to stop your thoughts; they will cease on their own when you become complete within that wholeheartedness. They just stop by themselves. If you try to stop them, that would be suppression and not a good thing. But even if they don't stop, it's okay because you see them as peripheral, on the sidelines. When you are down there, thoughts don't really matter.

So we learn to live with our basic nurturing instincts, in a more homely way. We begin to base ourselves there rather than in our thoughts, and then we find that even our thoughts begin to change in their nature into a much better form. We can bring about a great deal of change within ourselves without a great deal of concentrated effort. It doesn't require effort – just a quiet casual way of doing things, but with full attention.

If you find you are too serious, let that go, because it will lead to trouble. You want a light-heartedness, which is open rather than closed. Concentrated thought closes your mind; it's not open to receive anything, it merely contains what is there. But if it's completely open, then it has a passage in and out and it's not necessary to grasp and stop it. That's what we need – information coming in and out but not necessarily held, so we can be familiar with things but not necessarily possess them or be possessed by them.

If you collect a lot of things, do you possess them or do they possess you? They possess you – that's why you have to insure them against being stolen or harmed or damaged. Legally, we may buy and own things, but in ethical and moral terms it's a different thing altogether. We have the use of things for a limited period of time, but they can never wholly be our possessions. Why? Because my physical body is only impermanent. It will die. Who possesses these things then? Consciousness does not need them. They are merely for the body's use, whilst it's here temporarily.

An Exercise

There is another exercise you can play with: wherever you are, look straight across the room opposite you. It doesn't matter what object you look at – just fix your eyes to the object, and see that there is you and there is that. Be aware of the duality between you and it. Now, without moving your head, or your eyes, take your attention off that object and gradually bring it around to the periphery, so that you become aware of everything around the object, and eventually so that you can see the whole room in your vision...

Now tell me where duality is, and where you are in relation to it. Now there is only the room, with no me.

The Ego

Self only exists through the unsatisfactory. It does not live through the satisfactory because that involves union. The self requires separateness, to prove its existence.

This is why many people can't sit down for long; they have to get up and be doing, to reinforce the 'I am'. This is the discomfort zone. On the basis of unsatisfactoriness, we seek more unsatisfactoriness, because if we lose that, we lose self.

This comes from not knowing what self really is. The self is trying to reinforce something which it is not. It doesn't realise that in a sense it is not a thing at all. It is a spirit.

That spirit covers everything. Therefore it can't be separate. It can't take the aspect of 'I and another.' Whatever it sees is part of itself, of the oneness. To a degree, in the conditioned area, the self is frightened of this oneness because it means that the separate I does not exist. It means death. The I is afraid of dying. But there is nothing to fear. The dying only takes place because there is a separate one. When there is the realisation that "I am deathless", death cannot take place. The self does not need a body any more.

That is its innate knowing – although it's not strictly knowing, but appreciation. Thought-knowing doesn't exist there, because there is no thought in the not knowing. Once that realisation dawns, the self can't go back to separation any more. It realises that bodies will always involve separation, but it is not the body. It is the consciousness that links everything together, as one.

In the same way, there may be a rapport in a group; it is felt to be quite comfortable and whole, even though we see separate bodies. As long as we don't think separately, we feel as one. Is that not true? We are as one in spirit. Only in physicality do we see separation, which is fragmentation.

Someone might feel that there is something missing, but as a person they are the bit that is missing from the whole (laughs). Big joke really, isn't it?

You might say that the cart is pushing the horse rather than the horse pulling the cart. The intelligent being is the spirit, the ignorance lies in the physical being. But the physical being believes it is intelligent – the opposite of the truth! As spirit the self is a loving, nurturing thing. As an entity in physicality, it is at war with everything. So when you look at the nature of physicality, seek out its opposite and you will find it within yourself. There you are touching into the spirit. That which is manifest is a reflection in opposition to that which really is.

Alcoholism and Awakening

I was in an alcohol treatment centre, at 38 years of age. I was searching for something, I did not know what, and the alcohol treated my illness. I was irritable, restless, discontented, but with a bottle of brandy I was fine. I am still very ignorant in many fields, but I have had several insights, one of which saved my life. Some people with my illness, alcoholism, never have that insight, even though they are more intelligent than me. Who, or what, decides who receives the insight and who doesn't?

I think – and perhaps at a later date you may see this for yourself – that when you compare yourself with the others, there is a 'bent' in a particular direction which they don't have. And that bent is not for physicality at all. It is something of a different nature. You are not wholly aware of what it is, but you feel there is something there which you have to discover. Now this indicates that previous lives have been working in that direction, towards what you have today. It may well be the very thing that drove you to alcohol.

I can only describe myself in this respect: early on there was something I knew I ought to know. I did not know what it was; I didn't know how to look for it and it was very frustrating. The more I searched, the more frustrating it became. It could easily have led me to alcohol, but fortunately it didn't. The war came along, and took me in a different direction. The problem was postponed, and as a result of certain experiences during that time, it settled in another way.

That frustration could lead to alcoholism. And alcohol is very insidious, of course – once you're into it, it takes you over. But underlying it, the urge to find something else is still there. Now because of the previous lives which have brought you into this one, when you were between death and birth there was a reassessment in consciousness as to what was required in your birth, which put you into the area where you are now. And the compulsion to follow this unknown thing drove you to frustration, to the bottle. That helped to take pressure off, and you were stuck with it. But in your case the urge was so powerful – because of how far you had come in your previous lifetimes – that it even broke through that and drove you to the realisation that this is not the way to go. So you found the way out of it.

Previous innate memory – when it is powerful enough – penetrates through and guides you without knowing why. Now all you need to do is to let it happen. You've done all the hard work. Just leave it all behind now, and allow yourself to gradually open out and see more clearly. You don't have to work too hard at it – just quietly dwell on the nature of things. This is understanding through the sense of gut feeling rather than thought aspects, and gradually you begin to feel more in that respect. You feel, "I know," even though you couldn't necessarily tell yourself, or anybody else, what you know. You don't have to do very much at all, just ponder things as they arise and let them reveal their nature. Don't try pursuing anything deliberately – the more you push it, the more you push it away. Just quietly contemplate it – quietly, gently, more relaxed – until it gives up what it has. Or maybe leave it again for another day, as the case may be. But be patient and gradually it will all be revealed to you, rather than you seeking it out.

You have done the work necessary for this to happen. You have climbed the mountain. You are coming down the side now, freewheeling. Allow yourself to freewheel and enjoy the scenery as you go. You don't have to make any great effort at all. Open up, relax. Let it happen and you'll find it comes.

What you will find now is that you're beginning to recognise the nurturing spirit within rather than the one outside. It is within you coming out, not outside you coming in. Gradually, as you allow it to manifest, it will bring more and more peace to you.

And truthfully it is the only cure. The quiet dropping into the silent stillness is all that is required.

But just be patient and don't have any expectations. You won't have a glorious, sudden awakening; it will be ordinary-everyday. Perfectly ordinary. That's appropriate, because if you did have a huge awakening it might be too much for you to handle. As an enlightened person said long ago, it "creeps up like a thief in the night." (Laughs.)

The big joke about it is, when you have one or two little insights, they seem so simple and true, and you ask yourself, "How is it that I never saw it before?" It has been there all the time and you never saw it.

I think it is possibly a deep seated, self-centred ego that has deluded me.

Exactly. You're looking for something other than what it is. When it arrives, it is completely fulfilling in the moment of seeing. It's like walking down the street for many, many years without realising there are cracks in the pavement. You never saw what was there, because you were too busy looking for other things.

It's very much a question of slowing down. Don't push forwards, go slower, and you'll see more. Go too fast and you miss things. The trouble is that the world is speeding up and we get caught up in it. Slow down; begin to see more.

Chapter 10

Horses and Healing

This new state was odd, but one became attuned to it in a way that it wasn't other than itself. It was very difficult to explain. I'd never expected to experience anything like it. I thought about telling other people about it, but I realised that I couldn't. They'd think I was mad.

But it stayed with me. I felt like I wasn't myself anymore, and began to wonder if I really existed, because it was such a different existence. I had the same body, was still doing the same work, but with a completely different nature of mind. It was a new life, without a future.

I felt a sense of oneness towards everything. There is nothing which was not of the same nature. Now I can understand the Biblical aspect of this: in the beginning there was nothing – no thing, just emptiness. Out of that emptiness things began to materialise. That's why space is the most important quality in the whole universe.

I'd been looking for happiness but now I began to realise that happiness is delusion. It's based on having certain things, or achieving certain things. It depends on external circumstances, which can change at any moment. It is conditioned. But the contentment I found then – and still have now – is uncondi-tioned. It doesn't require anything. It doesn't matter what you have, or whether you have anything at all. Just to be is a state of well-being. In this state everything is interesting. You're never bored – everything is interesting because it's all a part of the same consciousness. And there's nothing selfish about this – we don't find contentment through gaining anything, but through losing ourselves.

At the same time we are never lonely – even if we're alone,

loneliness never arises because we see all things as part of ourselves. There is no separateness and no fear.

As we moved around, in and out of fields, there were some strange incidents. On one occasion, the chap who looked after the wild animals was crushed and had to go to hospital, so I took over his duties. At that time, there was a cage at the side of the ring, in which the wild animals performed. That was attached to a tunnel to their travelling quarters. Consequently one was able, first thing in the morning, to run them down into the big cage while you cleaned out their dens. That was the first job in the morning. So that's what I did. I opened up the gate to the big cage, and released the door to let them out. I pulled out the slides which kept them in separate compartments, so they had free access. So they all went down into the cage, and I shut the door and bolted it.

There was no one else about apart from me. Their dens were in an old grey carriage divided into three sections, with slides. One side of it was completely barred, but not solid. In the middle there was a little gate, about three-foot high and two-foot wide, which was usually bolted with a padlock. I unlocked it, opened up the door, and went in with a brush and started brushing up the old sawdust, working my way from one end to the other. I'm right in the corner, sweeping away, and suddenly I stop and look around – there's the male lion, halfway through the entrance at the other end.

"This time I've really had it," I thought. There he was, his front two paws already over the entrance and raising his third leg to come over. I thought, "I don't stand a chance." And the next thing I knew I was standing 10 feet outside the cage, watching the lion bringing his other legs in. The door was closed and the padlock was on, locked. To this day I don't know how it happened. It was as if I was teleported.

Later with this show, we wintered up on the clifftops on Flamborough Head in Yorkshire. There was a farm near the lighthouse there, which wasn't used much. A chap and I decided we would take the tent ropes and go down the cliff to gather some shellfish, while the tide was out. So we took some stakes, hammered them in at the top, threw the ropes down, and down we went, all the way, about 300 feet. We got quite a collection of shellfish in a little bag, but the tide was beginning to turn and a storm came up. We could see it coming towards us. I said to the other chap who was working with me, "You get up first." I waited for him to reach halfway up, then followed. He disappeared over the top, but then the rain started up, so heavy that the rest of the climb was very difficult. I managed to reach the top, and by that time, the rain was torrential, and there was thunder and lightning all around me.

I thought, "I'd better take shelter – we'll come back for the rope when it's finished."

I was about three paces over the clifftop when the lightning hit me. The weight of it hit the back of my shoulders and thrust me to the ground. The water was pouring all around me. As I went down, I watched the blue flames run all over my body, over the rain; blue light all over my body.

I still wasn't touched. I stood up and staggered a couple of yards, then I was hit a second time. Again, it was like a ton weight landing on me. I staggered to my feet again, walked a few paces, then I was hit a third time. I could see this chap sitting there with one leg over the fence, looking horrified. I staggered to my feet again, and we went across the field to take shelter in a building. I was shaken, but amazingly, not hurt at all.

When I began to put things together, I thought, "I'm not being allowed to die." I was being looked after. I almost died so many times – the times when I was pulled out of the River Thames, the times when the policeman pulled me out of the sea in Palestine, then when I was electrocuted on the airfield, and here on the clifftop. I didn't know what or why, but I felt that I was being kept alive for a reason.

Then there came a time when we went to Dublin, to the Theatre Royal, over Christmastime. On the way back, I loaded my luggage on to the boat, then went back on to shore. I left my identity card in my luggage, and the captain wouldn't allow me on without it, even though I'd already been on and off to load it. So I was stuck in Dublin for an extra couple of days, with no means of support, waiting, while the rest of the show went back to England. While I was there I found myself picking up a great deal of agitation from the horses. I was deeply disturbed. I couldn't understand what was going on. Something was distressing them very deeply. What the hell could it be?

Eventually I retrieved the identity card, and sailed over from Dun Laoghaire a few days later. I hitchhiked my way to our winter quarters, arriving about three o'clock in the morning and made my way to the stables. There was no light, but everything was familiar; I knew precisely where everything was. As I was walking through, something grabbed me by the ankle and threw me to the ground.

I'm fighting something in the dark, I can feel its fur. I find its neck and start squeezing it, and it gives in. I know animals – once they've given in, it's over. So I let it go, knowing it won't fight back. I find the hurricane lamp, light it, and realise I've been fighting a baboon – a chacma baboon. It was on a chain, enough to allow it to run around a few yards, but not long enough to reach the horses. I realised that was why the horses were distressed – a strange animal they couldn't understand. I was so bonded with them that I'd picked up their feelings from hundreds of miles away.

They decided they were going back to Ireland, but I left the show. I found my way back to London and found a job at Billy Smart's circus, as a groom. They gave me four horses to look after straight away. On my first day, I was having lunch in the canteen when there was a sudden commotion, because one of the grooms had been very badly mauled by a horse and taken to hospital. He was the fourth person this had happened to with this particular horse. I went to see what was happening, and young Billy Smart – Billy Smart's son – was about to put a whip to the horse. I said, "No, you don't do that."

"But he's mauled a man. It's the fourth time it's happened."

"You're not doing that. You'll only make it worse. If you want to chastise an animal, you've got to do it in the moment, otherwise they won't make the connection. As far as it goes, there's no such thing as a bad horse. I'll take it on, in addition to the four others I've got, and I guarantee that within 24 hours I'll have it like a kitten. And if I don't, you can use the whip on me."

The horse's name was Mephisto, a big black Friesian horse, a stallion – a lovely animal. I went into his stall, and he turned towards me, lifting his head and baring his teeth. I held up my finger as if to say "No" and gave a sign that I would retaliate if necessary. I walked up to his nose, patted it, showing him I was a friend, not foe. I breathed into his nostrils, quietly and gently, so we were exchanging breath. He accepted me straight away; I could sense him calming down. I rolled my hand over his body, gently stroking his legs and each foot. Inside half an hour, everything was at peace.

Later the same day, Mephisto slipped his collar. Nobody had told me, but he did that every so often. He was loose in the middle of the field; nobody would go near him. I walked up to him, and spoke to him – not in words as such. I had my own language which I used with horses. But I said to him, "Come on, Mephisto, what's all this about? You know you shouldn't be here. Come on, let's go back."

We walked back to the stall with his head over my shoulder, nuzzled in my ear. Then I made him a different kind of collar, so he couldn't slip it anymore.

Everyone was amazed. This horse which had put four people in hospital was acting like a kitten. Young Billy Smart said, "I don't know what you've done, but that's magic – I've never seen that before."

I introduced Mephisto to the other grooms, and he became quite amenable to them too.

One of the ringmasters at Billy Smart's circus was called Harold Holt, a real showman. He left the show shortly after I joined, when we moved on to Torquay. Shortly afterwards I received a telegram from Harold, saying, "Come to Haringey – we need you badly."

I decided to go, and when I arrived, Harold was organising the Rodeo show. They had made a corral out of eight-foot high fences, and brought about 27 wild horses over from the bogs of Ireland, horses which had never been touched by anyone before. They went straight out of the horsebox into the corral, with some water and some hay. They were very volatile; nobody knew how to handle them. But Harold had seen me with Mephisto and wanted me to do the same with these horses.

I walked into the corral with a bucket of water, and sat and waited. After an hour or so, one of them came up to drink some water from the bucket, and I let him drink it. I sat there completely calm and quietly – he took a few sniffs, and accepted me. I did that for two days, and one by one, each horse came up to drink, and sniffed me, and accepted me. I managed to get head collars on them all, and into the stables. After those two days, they were all working with me, not against me.

I did the same with about 150 wild horses that season; about the same the following season. One of the riders told me, "There's nothing that you can't put right. I've seen a few things go wrong, but when you touch them, they all go right again."

So my attachment to the horses still worked. I found out that I could heal them too. A horse would go lame in the afternoon and by the evening they would be back in the arena. Horses often had twisted ankles, and I would heal them with a kind of manip-ulation, a kind of massage – but perhaps a type of spiritual healing too. I couldn't explain it – it was just a touch I had.

I have done it with people too. Years later, at the Buddhist Society in Manchester, there was a girl who worked with my friend Connie, who went out walking in the Peak District, and hurt her ankle so badly that she could hardly stand up. I worked on her, used the same kind of massage and manipulation I did with the horses, and by the following day she was back at work. That evening she even went dancing.

I had a magic quality with horses, a special rapport. One time up at Sunderland, we let the horses out into a paddock, surrounded by chestnut fencing, strips of wood with wire holding them together. The horses had a free run, but unfortunately some youngsters who'd had a few drinks started chasing them. One of the horses tried to jump the fence and impaled itself on one of the strips of wood. It ploughed right through his brisket, a huge nasty cut, so wide and deep you could put your hand in it. The horse was so distressed that he wouldn't let the vet touch him. The vet was going to put a twitch on it, but I said, "No, you're not going to do that, not to one of my horses. You tell me what to do and I'll do it."

"Don't be a fool," he said. "You won't be able to do this."

I sat myself down in front of the horse, with one leg through his legs. The vet gave me a packing needle and some catgut to make stiches every half-inch, and a plastic straw for the bottom of the cut, to make sure that as it heals the surplus pus will drain out.

It took about an hour and a half. I used a pair of pliers to put big tacks into the cut. It was hard work, putting the needle through horse hide with pliers. It must have been very painful for the horse – every now and then he put his head down on the back of my neck, to rub his chin against the back of my neck, telling me that it was hurting but that I could keep going.

The vet was amazed. "I've never seen anything like that in my life."

There was a similar incident when we were on a tenting show. We let the horses loose in a field, but didn't know there was broken glass in a corner of it. I looked up and saw that one of the horses was limping very badly. The glass was embedded in its hoof and it was screaming in pain. It wouldn't stand still for anyone, until I arrived. I calmed it down, and it became still enough for me to lift up its hoof. It was difficult, because you can't see glass in blood, but the horse was so calm that I was able to feel gently around with my fingers, until I found the pieces and picked them out.

It was wonderful to have that rapport with the horses. Once you've bonded with them, they trust you completely. I saw that very clearly at the end of the season, when we were in Salford. We put the caravans behind some hoardings opposite the theatre, and I stayed with the horses in an old garage at the back of the theatre. We arrived on the Sunday, bedded the horses down with straw, put up the hay net, and a rope around them to tether them, and they were nicely settled down. Then we closed it off and went back to the caravan for a meal.

Then a little boy comes out: "Mister, there's a fire – your horses are on fire." Someone had thrown a firework through an open window, and set the straw alight. In those days I used to carry a knife, a sheath knife with a six-inch blade. I ran in there and went round cutting the horses free. There was no time to untie anything, so I just sliced the ropes. None of them tried to run away. They just stood there and waited, until every horse was cut loose. Then I called them outside, and they walked out with me, with bits of rope stuck to their head collars. I kept talking to them all the way through and not one of them bolted, even with the fire engines and all the noise, and the people running to and fro. They just stood with me until it was over. That's trust for you. One of them, a Shetland pony, did get a bit burnt – I had to throw my coat over it to stop the fire. It was badly blistered. We had to knock a chemist up for some olive oil to put on the burn.

I felt a rapport with people too, but in a different way. People are deceptive; they even deceive themselves. I can sense the true nature underlying their personalities, and that true nature is wonderful. But the terrible thing is that their minds are full of chaos and brutality. They're not what they really are. When you see a little kitten, your first instinct is to respond with love, kindness. That's how I respond to everybody, even though there's a tinge of sadness, because of their inability to see their own true nature.

One of the first times I saw that clearly was in Blackpool, where I went for a season after the rodeo in Haringey. It was a Sunday, and I was in a pub having a drink with some of the folk from the show. We were in a room in the pub, and a girl popped her head around the door, as if she was looking for a friend. I looked up and glanced at her; and suddenly, for the first time I saw the light within, in a human being. It was wonderful, a revelation, seeing this radiance inside her, something that was totally different to her surface personality.

I began to see it in other people too – a spark of spirituality deep within. For some people it's faint, like a glowing ember, but for others it's very bright.

Chapter 11

Spiritual Development

Do you think the different stages of spiritual development overlap?

Yes, definitely, there is no marked point of moving over. There is an overlapping which takes place which you can only become aware of when you are past the point of change. You can sometimes trace a change back to where it actually happened, but that's very difficult. This is spiritual rather than physical, so the lines of demarcation are very vague. But you reach a point where things of a beneficial nature take place within you, and similar things arise in that total conscious area of the spirit. Gradually you find that a greater transparency develops, which indicates moving off into another dimension, until the transparency fades away altogether and it's just a total unity. And that of course is another area altogether, moving from the heavenly into the celestial realms. These are very difficult to talk about at all, except for one factor: all the while through the physical realms, through hell and heaven states, there is a degree of duality. However, in the celestial realms the transparency becomes so clear that duality disappears into a total unity. It still retains its conscious identity – rather than self-identity – but with the realisation that it has never been born.

Now that is a strange thing to say, isn't it? You and I are here with a physical aspect, assuming that we were born. But consciousness was never born into this body; it became attached to it. It was never born as the body, which is why it can eventually leave it.

When did it enter the body?

It didn't enter the body, it became attached to the body. So it is both in and out of the physical, but not a part of it at all. That's why you can sense or feel physical things, even within the physical body. Of course, this is a construct, not a reality. The feeling is one thing, but we grasp at it, create a conceptual world out of it, a delusory world, and deceive ourselves that we are something we're not. The truth is we were always and always will be pure consciousness, which was there before the world began and will be there when it's gone. That is very hard to take in, of course. But at some point you will find it to be true yourself.

You'll reach a place which is beyond words. That's the problem: if you were a fish and were able to talk, would you be able to make yourself understood here? You wouldn't, because all the concepts and ideas wouldn't make sense. The same thing applies to us in the spiritual element. Our meanings come from our conditions, but in the spiritual element there are no conditions whatsoever, so how do you explain it? We only know what the conditioned means until duality ceases and we break away and see the reality.

Generally speaking, therefore, what we talk about in words is not wholly true. Truth lies in experience, not in any thoughts or ideas about experience. It's like hitting your thumb with a hammer when you're putting a nail in a wall – then you know what pain is. But you couldn't explain that pain to somebody else, unless they have the same experience. You have to experience it to know it.

Practices such as meditation and chanting can take you away from the conditioned world temporarily, which gives you a chance to appreciate the difference between the conditioned and the unconditioned. And what you find, in deep meditation for instance, is a void which is beyond measure and beyond dimensions. Consciousness expands way beyond the body – in fact, it isn't even conscious of the body, only this vast, boundless emptiness.

Keep going there – don't try to see anything, but keep the mind's eye open. Sooner or later things will arise and show themselves to you. And in that showing you will experience unity, because what arises is absorbed into the consciousness. Perhaps there will be a time when you're quietly doing something in a state of absorption, and suddenly you *know*; suddenly it takes your breath away. But not in meditation – meditation only prepares the ground.

You can only deal with these things by looking at your own experience. Don't look to my experience as a given truth – your truth is what matters, not mine. And when you begin to see things you'll find they're not so different anyway – but at least you know for sure, through experience rather than through a belief system. Belief prevents you from seeing the actual.

When you see the true nature of things, you realise that it is both your own and that of the whole universe. It is one nature, and this is where the *metta* aspect comes in again: being total, complete, without separateness – this means love. And when we are able to access that, and to live in the world with it, there is nothing we can give to the world but loving-kindness – because that is all we are.

There are various ways of showing it, of course. The body and the mind pick up many habit patterns over a lifetime, and a lot of these will continue, as conditions which have nothing to do with you. You used to think the conditions were you, because you were closely attached to them. They aren't you anymore, but they still continue. I still wear a tie. Why? Because I've been doing it all my life *(laughs)*. No other reason – it's just a habit pattern. But conditions give us an apparent identity.

The Emotions

The apparatus of emotion can feel very expansive. Can metta have an emotional aspect?

We have to be careful about this. The emotions are a very necessary factor whilst we live in the body. When you experience mental agitation, it's like a glass of water with a lot of ripples in it. If you look into the glass you see a distorted image of what is there, because of the ripples. And you don't realise the ripples are there – you assume the distorted image is real, and you act upon your apparent understanding of it.

This is what has been going on throughout your life. But when the agitation – which is caused by grasping and aversion – begins to cease, then the mind becomes smoother, a mirror-like surface, and now you see a true picture, the situation as it really is. Living in the moment, there is now a clarity – in the seeing is the knowing, in the experiencing is the knowing. You can therefore respond if necessary – or not, if there is no necessity.

So even once they have been stilled, emotions do play a part. For the first time they make their play in a proper manner; things are seen clearly without distortion. Having eliminated the grasping and aversion aspects, we've also eliminated the whole conceptual field. We see clearly, with no judgement whatsoever. There is nothing to judge by, because judgement lies in a conceptual field. And if that field is clear and empty, then no judgement can take place. It is so utterly simple – things don't need to be understood because they can be seen wholly, not partially.

All kinds of understandings are built on partial information; that's why they change. As different criteria are seen, they alter your understanding. But when you see things clearly for what they are, understanding isn't necessary. With other people, for instance, you see their natures for what they are; you see what they can respond to and what they can't. You don't assess it, just see it clearly. Consequently you're able to deal with their needs at their level rather than at your own. So gradually, step by step, you can take them further along, stretch their mind a little bit at a time, so that they're expanding their understanding – *initially* their understanding, which is what we have to work with. We gently guide them into comprehending these feelings, in experience; and then gradually, they begin to progress from understanding to knowing. With knowing, there is no baggage –

the moment is known without any reference to the past. It just is, and that is the completeness of the whole thing.

It's very strange, I try to explain these things as best I can but this 'thing' that talks about these various aspects, as I have been doing tonight – it's not me. It just comes through at any given point in time and I have no control over it whatsoever. I don't carry any knowledge about it whatsoever. It comes through and I listen to it the same as you do, and then it's gone again.

What struck me is that at one end you have the emotional expression of metta, which isn't really metta, and at the other end you have grief, loss, and other negative emotions. But the spectrum is actually quite narrow and limited.

Yes, but when you really look at this what you see is that there is a great deal of falsity. Emotional feelings can be moments of utter delight, or of utter despair. Opposites – but the basic feeling is precisely the same. The only difference is content of the mind. There is only a disturbance, which we decide is good or bad as the case may be.

I did that yesterday. I felt really out of sorts, and suddenly I thought that if I could be at peace with where I am now, then it would be irrelevant what state I was in. And all of sudden there was a bird flying by and I could see the feathers on its wing. The body still felt uncomfortable but the mind wasn't reacting to the discomfort anymore.

This is the truth of what the Buddha taught: "What is the motivation for doing anything at all?" The answer is: I am not content with where I am. I want to be something else. I want to get something else. I want to get rid of something, because I am not comfortable. If I were comfortable here, would I move from this chair to that because that one appears to be more comfortable?

Unsatisfactory situations within oneself are the cause of everything. If we knew precisely who or what we were, we would be content with that. We wouldn't want to go anywhere and we wouldn't need to pursue any ambitions. If you were content would you do anything in particular?

So we're not wholly content, and that's why we pursue other things, to alleviate our discontent. Discontent is the ruling factor behind our activity. Unfortunately, since we don't see it very clearly, all we know is that we're not very comfortable, and something else looks more comfortable, so we go and chase that, or we possess it, and hope that we'll feel better. Perhaps we do for a little while, but since we have taken our discomfort to the new situation, it turns to discomfort as well. So the whole of life is discomfort, moving from this to that, to that, to that, like a grasshopper.

The whole point is to eliminate those factors that cause the dissatisfaction, which truly speaking is our concept of duality: "I am lonely," therefore I need some sort of company; "I'm not whole, there is something missing in my life." As I've already mentioned, there's nothing missing in your life; it was always there, you just never saw it. You looked into duality instead of the fullness of wholeness itself.

The very factor of not being content is the source of all of our problems. Since we have a conceptual area of duality, we assume that something is missing, and therefore we have to add to it. In the conditioned world, all these things are subject to change, as is the self. So this world is never going to be wholly satisfactory, and you're just building more discontent on discontent upon discontent to make it worse. The answer is to go deep down within, and ask yourself, "Why am I discontent?"

Now if you look deep down you find there is no discontent at all. There is just an idea that has become a problem.

Let me put it another way – in a short while, here, we may all feel as one and become contented. And we don't have to do anything; we just need to let things go. It's a very hard lesson to learn, that we don't have to do anything, just *let* things happen.

We have to face up to our so-called problems, not run away from them. We must meet them where we stand, if possible. No matter what they may appear to be, they can't be stronger than you. Why? Because you are the one who created them in the first place.

Making Spiritual Progress

How can one know when one is making spiritual progress?

You can't. It's only when a situation shows you that you have changed that you realise. At all points, no matter where you are in your life, it is normal. The normality changes but you don't notice it.

You realised you've changed by noticing what you've lost, not what you've gained. For instance, you might recall that, earlier on, you used to get angry very quickly about certain things. But now when similar things happen you find you don't get angry at all. You've lost the grasping at that situation that made you get angry, or at least it has weakened. These are the things that show us we've progressed, but unless the situation arises we don't become aware of the progress. You don't realise something is lost until you realise you want it and find that it's not there *(laughs)*. That's why it's difficult. You could be well along the path and not know it, unless some little incident shows you, "I used to be like that and I'm not anymore." It could be a long time before that situation arises. That's why it's known as a gradual path *(laughs)*. Other people may see it but you yourself don't.

I agree entirely with what you are saying, but sometimes when you're being mindful, you know you are letting go of something and it feels a little bit like you are losing something.

That's right and you're not too sure what it is. You can't be certain, until something really remarkable – something more intense – shows you. That's why it is so necessary to have a group where you can compare notes, to share what's happening to you and gain understanding. But it's true that with a sharpened aspect of awareness you can see these things, and be aware of an impending change even before it happens, though you don't know what it is yet. It's almost as if you're waiting for something to happen. You're touching into the truer levels of consciousness, which have a wider expanse than normal consciousness, so you can reach into the future and sense that something is going to occur.

You also become much more aware of the subtle manifestations, particularly greed and hatred. I sometimes think I feel hatred, but when I actually compare it with a few years ago, it's just a subtle annoyance. Yet you have become more starkly aware of it.

The curious thing is that where these emotions arise you see them as conditioning and not of yourself. And you can decide whether to pick them up or to leave them be. This is where you find you have choices – you can either pick them up and go back into the world, or you can leave them behind and go forward. That is your choice. Usually you go forward – going back isn't worthwhile. And this happens without a single thought, strangely enough. The choice is made by consciousness.

Dealing with Pain

What is the best way to deal with pain?

The body can know pain, but *you* don't have to know it. I've recently been experiencing that myself. There has been pain, but that doesn't mean I've suffered it. It's almost as if consciousness is an entity in its own right, separate from the body. It has its own life. We communicate with one another through the body in this world, but we also communicate in consciousness, all the time, regardless of the presence of the body. This is not physical contact, but spiritual contact.

Consciousness is what I am, not who I am. There is a big difference. The real entity is the consciousness, not me being conscious. If you can experience that, only then will you realise a degree of contentedness, because then there is nothing missing. All is well with the world.

According to Buddhism, in order to achieve peace we have to

rid ourselves of desires and aversions, and all our sensual perceptions. You can't drink alcohol, can't have sex – you can't have this, you can't have that. But in actual fact, as you develop, the opposite occurs. Experience broadens rather than narrows. Everything which arises is interesting – infinitely interesting. Since there is less thinking about things, there is more experiencing of life, so in fact one begins to live life to the full for the first time. Interesting isn't it? One lives life to the full for the first time because one is attuned to everything in the moment that it arises. Therefore there is contentedness, because there is union with everything. Hard to believe, isn't it? That is the truth of the matter.

So when you extinguish all these conditions, you find that you're entering into a different field altogether, because all these discomforts are weighed down with the conditions. If you remove the conditions the discomforts disappear. What are you left with? Since you are not dead, there is no condition to produce any sort of discomfort, so you must be comfortable. It goes without saying, doesn't it?

I feel attached to things like the wind and the trees and the water and the sky, and the physical senses. Does all that have to go as well? I enjoy it.

I would question whether you are attached to these things. When you look at them you are at peace within yourself. So it's the peace that you're looking for. And you can't cling to peace. You pay attention to these phenomena – the wind or the trees – and find them restful. And you can't have rest at the same as clinging to something. You have to relax, and become as one with them, so there is no attachment whatsoever. That is the natural state of consciousness, to be at one with everything in its consciousness. It's so perfectly natural that you don't have to do it.

As you go further along with this, you find it can be done by just letting go of things which annoy you, and looking for things which don't. The quiet stillness that arises in these situations is the most important factor in your life. And if you learn to live within the body rather than in the head – if you deal with everything which arises and act from the heart rather than the head – then you'll find that the stillness remains with you in other situations. It is a whole body experience, not a mental experience.

I also need to let go of aversions.

Don't worry too much about the things you are averse to – try to accept them. Leave them be and they won't do any harm.

The Importance of Humour

All the while we try to lighten the load *(laughs)*. It's a joyful thing, not a heavy thing. The more you laugh about it, the better. The more you play with it the better. Don't be too serious – play with it, and enjoy the play. Where else does joy come from apart from play? If you become too serious you get bogged down and fall into depression. If you are light-hearted you absorb things. In the play you learn far more than through being serious. In depth, in experience – that's how we learn. Granted, this is the most serious thing you ever did in your life, but it doesn't have to be handled that way. Do it with fun, make it fun.

Humour is a mark of spirituality. If somebody is too straight-laced, they have no spirituality. Spirituality begins with light-heartedness, a feeling of buoyancy and joy.

This always bothered me about religion. As a boy, I was brought up in the Church of England, and it was always straight-laced. If religion is supposed to be a joyful thing – I thought to myself – why weren't these people enjoying themselves? Even today, they're still not enjoying themselves. They're still too straight-laced. When you're straight-laced you are tense. When you are tense, mentally, physically or emotionally, you can't learn, no matter how hard you try. But when you are open and light-hearted, you can absorb almost everything.

So light-hearted buoyancy is what we require, to allow these things to arise from within – and some from without. You have a door that is always open, in both directions. It is all balanced. You can't do it when you are deliberate. That just closes the doors to any kind of learning. Just be open and enjoy. It is a very simple way of looking at it, but it's absolutely true. You can do so much in a jocular fashion that you can't in seriousness. A serious manner weighs you down.

If you're getting tense, relax. The whole world is full of tension – that's why it's in trouble.

Chapter 12

Confirmation

Living was only a means to an end – the end being to live in a different dimension, a conscious dimension which is completely and utterly different and can't be explained to anybody. It was like being born all over again, living a new life.

Once I'd settled into this new state – which took a while – I felt I had something very valuable which people should know about. I was travelling around and tried to explain what I was experiencing to local vicars and clergymen. I told them I only saw wholeness, with no separation, this natural state of being which was nurturing and kindness. I thought it would interest them, but they didn't understand. They thought it was far-fetched, or that I was being blasphemous.

I was dealing with it from a heart point of view, while they were coming from an intellectual perspective. They couldn't communicate on my level, and I couldn't on theirs, so we were talking at cross purposes. They were dealing with belief, while I was talking about the reality of experience – so it was totally different. This went on for a few years, until I realised there was no point, and stopped approaching people.

Christianity seemed false to me. As a child, I went to Sunday school, where they read passages and stories from the Bible, and knew deep within they didn't know the true meaning of them. It was only words, which are just symbols of something deeper, something they didn't have access to. Here I was experiencing no separation, other than physical – a feeling of oneness with everything. The true meaning of the church term 'holy communion'.

It should never be a question of praying for anything, but of giving thanks for what one is. From a traditional church point of view, the whole business is to get something from someone else –

when in actual fact we already have everything, so there is nothing to be asked for.

The lack of understanding from others had the effect of making me very confused. I had a lot of knowledge but I couldn't communicate it to anybody. I began to doubt myself. I thought, "If nobody can appreciate this, I must be mad. I'm so different to everybody else." I knew deep down that I wasn't mad, that I had something that was profoundly important to other people, but it was overlaid with this confusion.

By this time I was back in London – I came back after the season in Blackpool, and found a job straight away as a lifeguard at the swimming baths in Islington. I had a garret room in Finsbury Park, and one night I was sitting up there, pondering over it all, feeling upset and frustrated. The frustration grew in intensity inside me, until I shouted out, "For God's sake, somebody help me!"

The next moment there was a massive flood of peace, a vast emptiness full of love. There was no substance. It was the same serene feeling I'd had before with the horses, but in greater depth. It was as if someone had dropped a soft warm blanket over me.

It stayed with me for three days. I asked if I was allowed to know who or what was responsible for the flood of peace and a man's face appeared in my mind's eye – a foreign face, dark-skinned, possibly Indian. My only thought was, "I've never seen such a sweet, beautiful face on a man in all my life." There was such benevolence in it. He was grey-haired, with a beard, and the most beautiful eyes, full of love and benevolence. I didn't know who he was at the time.

Just three days later, I was working at the baths as usual, and a storm blew up, with lightning and thunder. I travelled back to my room in Finsbury Park, and did something I'd never done before – I bought an evening paper on the corner of the street.

"What did I get this for?" I was thinking. I opened it at a page full of adverts all the same size, and one jumped out, about somebody who was giving a lecture on spiritual healing in Holloway, about four miles away. Even with the dreadful weather, I felt impelled to go.

I arrived there like a drowned rat, while the lecture was already underway. It was a church hall, about a dozen people present, and I sat in the back row. There was a man two chairs in front of me, making notes on a pad. When the lecture was over, the speaker asked for any questions, and this man in front of me stood up and gave him a massive dressing down, even worse than I'd heard in the army. The intensity was amazing.

"This isn't spiritual healing," he said. "You should never attempt to teach people about spiritual healing. You don't know what you're talking about." Then he suddenly turned round to me and said, "I suppose you're the reason I've come here this evening, aren't you? It certainly wasn't for that."

There was a coffee shop just a couple of doors down, and we were there until 2 o'clock in the morning. He asked me various questions, all related to Buddhism, and he was amazed by my answers. "How do you know all this?" he asked.

"I just know."

"But how did you come to know? This is all pure Buddhism."

He was John Garrie, one of the founders of the Buddhist Society of Manchester. He was the first person I ever met who could understand me. I could explain the way I experienced the world and he could relate it to the teachings of Buddhism. I felt a deep rapport with him. We decided we had to meet up again, and were together virtually every evening. I'd describe my experiences and he'd tell me which Buddhist sutta it fitted with.

It was a massive relief, to find out that I wasn't mad after all. I found out later that he'd been drawn to that meeting in a similar convoluted way to me. He had felt impelled to go too, even though he wasn't keen. I suspect that there was some degree of manipulation going on, perhaps in answer to my call for help.

John was a part-time actor, out of work, making a living as a painter and decorator. I learned a lot from him. He was quite a psychic, and we spent a lot of time investigating various psychic phenomena, going to séances, spiritual healers, and so on. All very interesting but not spiritual. He was able to reduce his pulse rate to almost nothing, like an Indian Yogi. And he was one of the best healers I've met in my life. We were experimenting one time in his flat and he was telling me about his healing powers. We all smoked in those days; I burned the back of my hand with a cigarette and said, "Do something with that."

He traced a circle around the burn, and the pain disappeared straight away. Then he held his hand over the mark – my hand went ice cold, and you could see the redness slowly fade away. Within 15 minutes it had gone, without leaving a scar.

Whilst I was at the baths the manager's wife, who lived up above the baths, had a whitlow on her finger – very painful, swollen to the size of three fingers, wrapped up in a bandage. It was so painful that she wouldn't touch it. I told her, "Look, I've got a friend who might be able to help – although he's not a doctor." She didn't care, was willing to try anything, so I brought John along the very same evening. He took a look and said, "I'm going to take the bandage off now, and it won't hurt, trust me."

He held his hand around it, without touching, just for a few minutes, then put the bandage back on. He told her, "Now you won't feel pain anymore, and in the morning it will have gone."

"It's true – the pain's gone," she said. "It's not possible!" The next morning the whitlow had disappeared; she was astonished.

John had no idea how it was happening – he was just aware that a power was flowing through him.

Chapter 13

Becoming Still

An Exercise in Stillness

I have been trying to change gradually for a long time but it's as though I know the script but can't put it into action. The medicine is there – I look at it but I don't take it, or I just take a little bit of it, even though I know it is good for me.

You need the practice of being still. Here's an exercise you can play with – and I mean *play*, without being too serious:

Take a look at any part of your body – a finger or a toe, anything at all. Take a look at it and note that it's separate from the you that is looking. Now take a look at the table... It's also separate from the you that is looking. So is your body any different to that table? In both cases, you're really looking at an object, whether it is animate or inanimate.

Now, have a look at your thoughts. They may be pleasant, unpleasant, whatever they may be – but are they you?

No. All we have is a process that is going on, that's producing thoughts, good, bad or indifferent. But no part of it is you. From this, one has to draw the obvious conclusion that what *is* me is the looker, the one who is watching, the consciousness.

If I were honestly conscious would I be thinking these thoughts? Would I need them if I were fully conscious of what I am looking at? Would I need to think about it?

Now, if you examine the nature of that which is looking, the consciousness, I think you will find that in all circumstances, whatever it is viewing, it is serene, untroubled, at peace.

So, in this area, there is stillness, not busyness, do you follow? Have a little look at things in that light, and come to be still. You don't have to think about things, just see that they are going on.

That's sufficient. You don't have to define anything, just observe that things are changing all the time. And the one thing that's not changing is the viewer, the consciousness. It doesn't change – it remains serene, in all circumstances. Everything else goes up and down, forwards and backwards, whatever it may be, but never at rest. Whereas consciousness is always at rest.

Is it not possible that that consciousness is you, in the true sense, because what you consider to be you, as a self, is changing from moment to moment – angry this minute, undisturbed the next? It can be greedy, it can be hateful – it's me, but which one is me? Yet consciousness is always constant. Is that not the better one to be?

And it is always there, always there. If you can only transfer from the troubled to the untroubled.

That is right, because the sun is always shining.

Exactly – regardless of whether there is a cloud underneath. See yourself as the sun and not the cloud. You've been doing the opposite – regarding yourself as the cloud and not the sun.

Dealing with Difficulties

I have had a lot of difficulties.

Then a lot of the difficulties will disappear. It doesn't mean to say you won't have little problems that arise from time to time, but they can be dealt with quite easily. If you look back in your life, I am quite sure that, like everybody else, you've been up against obstacles which seemed almost insurmountable at that time, great troubles. But looking back now, you think, "What was I so concerned about? It was nothing." Your problems today are of a similar nature. Often you only need to let issues rest for a while and they will cure themselves. One of the conditions of the world is time, and time is constantly moving, so that anything that arises within the world cannot be sustained. As time moves on, all things dissolve away. That's why most seeming problems don't need touching at all. Just leave them be and they will fade away.

The cause of all this is concepts. If we had no concepts there would be no judgments. Therefore your emotions could act spontaneously as and when required, merely to show you the nature of things and nothing else, without you suffering. Emotions are useful, because they give you clues as to the nature of what you are dealing with. Provided they are not too active, so long as they are gently moving along, there is no problem with them. If there is no concept of what is right, wrong, bad, or indifferent, then they do not become too disturbed, and consequently they do their proper job, which is to reflect that which is coming in. They don't have to be disturbing at all.

Concepts tell us: "Because of this I'm going to be fine, because of that I'm going to feel awful," and so on. But there is no "because of" at all, just "the way it is." And it's perfectly alright the way it is; there is no problem. It is only because we decide there is a problem that problems come to be.

We forget that what we all want is peace. And you don't need to go round all the snakes and ladders to find peace; you just to need to let go of things.

You're perfectly right. We're motivated to look for peace or comfort by doing or gathering things, in the hope that they will bring us what we need. But they won't. You have to look for peace in here, not out there.

Whatever it is you want, practise it now. If you want peace start being peaceful now. Don't go looking for it tomorrow; it won't be there. It's now. If you want to be happy, start being happy now. If you find that the mind is drawn to things which create unhappiness, don't let it go there. Stay cool, and you'll find you are happy, content, without needing anything. Imagine yourself at the end of a day soaking in a nice warm bath. You relax, the mind relaxes, the body relaxes. Everything relaxes and you are content. Why can't you do it when you are not in the bath? Just stop doing things – that's all you need to do *(laughs)*.

The trouble is, we have conditioned ourselves over many, many lifetimes – including this one – to keep busy doing things, instead of being inactive. But you don't have to do. You can respond to things, but you don't have to go seeking to do things. It is totally habitual. There is nothing there. The mind has been trained to be busy, that's all. We have to untrain ourselves. But at the same time, you don't do nothing. You are aware – that is doing something. Even if you seem to be sitting doing nothing, your eyes can be seeing and you are conscious of what you see; your ears are hearing and you're conscious of that, you are breathing, smelling, tasting… All these things are there. You don't have to think about them, just to be aware.

The main thing is to be aware of being comfortable within. If you can do that, you can observe things which come in and produce a little discomfort, and examine why they produce the discomfort. You can quietly observe them and then return to the comfort. It's surprising – the comfort in here is already out there with you in everything you see. This is the real nature of things: the comfortable area of being 'part of' rather than 'separate from'.

The main thing is that when these things are operative you have a buoyant attitude. You can't get depressed; you ride along as though you are on a cloud. Things don't bother you too much, which means you can see more clearly. So you can laugh much more easily *(laughs)*.

Grasping

I know what I need to do, and I find solace in the spiritual side of things.

Yes, but the spiritual side works in a different way. You can't grasp at it, which is what makes it difficult for you. You're used to grasping at things to prove yourself. No matter what you have, you will never be wholly content whilst you have the attitude of, "I could do with a little more." If you go to the gym and start lifting weights you develop big muscles. When you grasp at things you become good at grasping. When you take on things you become good at taking things on. And the more you do, the stronger this desire becomes. Whatever you work at becomes stronger. The only way to overcome it is *not* to work at it, but to allow it to atrophy, to fade away.

We tend to cling to the things that bring us suffering, but not the things which give us freedom. When you are reasonably happy, you're open-minded and would give anything away. But with a little depression, you close everything into yourself, and develop a bigger ego, because you're so aware of yourself. When you are happy you aren't aware of yourself; you're so open that you don't realise there is a self there. So being selfless means happiness. As long as you don't try to contain it and leave it wide open, you will always be content. It means that you can't get hurt, as if you're so soft that things just bounce off you, or you just absorb them. Whereas in the other mode, you're rigid and hard, so things strike against you and you do get hurt.

Usually we grasp at our sorrows and our pains. We cling to them and make them us. *I* am suffering. When you're content you don't register them – you're so open, at one with things, that there are no problems. If you look back over your life you'll find there have been quite a few of those periods of contentment. They are not forgotten, although the negative periods may stand out because they hurt more. Many people today have a dim view of themselves because they identify themselves with the hardships rather than the lighter side of life. Look closely, and you will see that the lighter side is there.

Many people don't seem to understand that you can sit back and be yourself, and be content without grasping for anything. In fact, you're better off being empty than being bombarded with information. Be empty, open, let things come and go. You can know what's going on but you don't have to make it your own. You can't do much about it anyway.

If a person really wants to be content within themselves, they have to stop clinging to things which they can't do anything about. We have a news media that will tell you about all the troubles in the world and we get emotionally involved with what's happening in China, South Africa, South America, wherever it may be. But if you can't do a damn thing about it, why take it on board? Let it be. You can't cure the whole world, so leave it be.

It might sound selfish, but it isn't, because the state you're in affects the people around you. If you're at peace, they'll be at peace. If you're worried, they're going to be worried. So be seemingly selfish in this respect – let it go, be content, and you'll find people around you become reasonably content as well because they are sharing your state. So is it really selfish?

One thing I have learned is that when you get very, very down, you get upset about evil in the world and just sit there and wallow in it. That's not very useful.

It's not useful to yourself or anybody else. It's much more useful if you're at peace. In a troubled state of mind, you can't be of benefit to anybody. It's only when you cool down that you're able to do things properly.

All states are the same – anger can come, it can remain inside you for a week, or even longer. But if you notice it arising it can go within a second, just like that, by not holding on to it.

This is something I have observed in myself recently. There comes a moment where you have a choice – you can either accept the old script and go into all those thoughts and feelings, or you can just say, "I accept it," and move on.

Accept it and it will go, just like dropping a hot brick. The moment you accept it should be so, it is gone. This is what mindfulness is about: noticing things arising before they become established so that you can let them go. If they get established, you're likely to cling to them.

How can you let suffering go?

Whatever arises, give it a little stand-off time, and it will disappear. As time changes, its nature will change too. Don't grasp at it and try to stop time; let time move on and let it fade. Learn to let it be.

This is one of the problems with modern technology – everything has to be immediate. It's better to let things rest. We used to have a saying, "Sleep on it." Very sound advice – don't react immediately, ponder it a little while and then answer. When we meet something new – or even something familiar, for that matter – we don't fully appreciate it until we have dwelled with it for a little while, perhaps a few hours or a few days. Then we begin to see it in a different light, through feeling rather than thinking. And it's our feeling that really matters.

Once you've dwelt with an issue for a while, you realise that what *appeared* to be the problem is only really the shadow of the problem. The real problem lies a little deeper, and once you deal with that, the whole issue disappears, and no longer repeats itself. So give yourself time; don't take action immediately – unless of course it is an emergency. Then of course you do act immediately – and in that case you find that you act with spontaneity rather than through thought. You act instinctively.

Once thoughts start, they generate feelings.

Not necessarily. In this area, you have the feeling before the thought. If a stranger comes to your door, you have a 'gut feeling' about whether they're honest or dishonest. This inner feeling, this instinct, is not emotion. It's almost nowhere, there in the middle of the body, nothing to do with emotion whatsoever.

The point about this is that we have to deal with the self, our own self, not with other people. That's the only thing in the world we can change. We can't change other people – we can perhaps advise them here or there, but they don't have to take the advice. It is up to them.

In many ways, if we're going to achieve any sort of contentedness within ourselves, we have to ignore the greater mass of people, even our friends at times, to do what we feel is right, rather than what they think is right. We have to learn to trust ourselves to know what is right. If you have 10 million people going the same way, it doesn't mean to say they are right. They could all be wrong. You can decide for yourself and live your own way in the right way, and be content rather than confused.

It is not difficult; it can be done. But it does require some simple little exercises to clarify our minds, to learn to respond to our gut feelings more than our heads. We have to keep revisiting the gut level. Usually it's quite still, doing nothing, so when we visit there we might be conscious of an empty nothingness, which is in fact very, very peaceful, quite homely in fact, almost as if it's pointing the way home. The more we live with that then the clearer the mind becomes, so that it can see the world more directly and clearly, without complications, so that life becomes much more simple. Then we begin to live a spiritual life, rather than a physical one, even though we still live in a physical world. We begin to live by ethical values that come from deep within rather than selfish ones which come from the head.

We are very much conditioned by other people around us, not just in thought, but in the mood of the moment. If someone is angry, we get angry; if they are irritated, we become irritated. In the same way, we affect other people with our moods. If I get angry, you get angry. The point here is that if we control our outgoings, then our incomings will be changed. It's like throwing a ball against the wall – it comes back to you and you catch it. We begin to learn that what we put out is what the world throws back, so we can control it, to some degree at least.

Nurturing

Ponder this: your own deep nature is that of nurture. If a kitten walked in here, what would you feel? You would feel like you wanted to pick it up and nurture it, true? And that is without a single thought taking place – spontaneous, therefore from the depth of your being. So is that not your true nature? You automatically have that nurturing feeling, a recognition that here is a fellow being that needs a little help. We feel it towards animals, even plants when they start to come through, and babies and children. But it's different when it comes to other adults – we don't trust them, because they've been hiding away, just as we've been hiding ourselves away, not being honest, presenting themselves as something they are not. We don't trust anybody to show their real nature, because we don't trust ourselves to show our own real nature. We have a degree of fear that they may see us for what we are. But there is still an underlying feeling of nurturing towards one another.

I can prove that we don't have to hide from one another. We can prove it this very evening, in fact – that we can be ourselves and be happy being ourselves. I will guarantee that before this night is out, you'll feel a rapport in this room with everybody in it. You'll feel there is nothing to hide, that everything is fine. You'll feel part and parcel of the whole, not separate, that you belong with this group. We're all emanating a sense of well-being, percolating through from each of us. There is nothing to fear. We can be ourselves, and being ourselves means to extend our love out to others, as they do to us. This is what love is. This nurturing is love. And that nurturing flows out and criss-crosses and merges until you don't know who is who.

If we can experience this rapturous containment as a group, am I wholly separate from you, or you from me? In feeling – not in thought – you'll find you don't know where one leaves off and the next one begins. There are different bodies, obviously, but the consciousness deep within us, the nurturing aspect, is wholly shared. It isn't all of us as separate things but as a whole, a big pool, and it is multiplied by the number of persons involved. You can feel this for yourself; you can't argue with your experience. What we think about it may not be wholly true because we are bound by our concepts and ideas, which have been present over many years, in relation to different criteria. But this is a reality, in itself.

Let us become more acquainted with our own true natures and we'll find that they are the same in everyone, if only they were prepared to allow them to show through. In that showing, we experience this intermingling and feel much greater confidence in ourselves as individuals as a result.

This is what Christians call "Holy Communion". It's a spiritual aspect, with consciousness as spirit. It permeates through your whole being. And this is a state that we should learn to become familiar with, because, when fully realised, this truth will break you free of all your other conditions. Those conditions don't need to be there: the grasping, the clinging, the hatred, the jealousy, the envy. They all disappear and leave you serene in your consciousness of spirit, which is this rapport. It's as easy as that, although it's not simple: it just requires you to visit this area more and more until you become so familiar with it that it becomes the base from which you work in the world. You find that you're able to concentrate your being into everything that you do.

The one thing we normally cannot do through our senses is to use any two at the same time. We can flit from one to another so rapidly that there is the illusion that we may be seeing and hearing simultaneously, but that's not really the case, because each of these aspects works in a different dimension. When I say dimension, I'm speaking in terms of vibratory elements. Sight is one vibration, sound is another, and the different elements never meet. They are always separate.

But strangely, when we are able to let go of all these conditioned aspects and enter in stillness into the deeper unconditioned aspect, we experience an expansion of consciousness in which it's possible for all the elements to join together, as one. Consequently, our appreciation of things becomes so different. Here is a piece of cloth, for example – to feel it gives you one dimension, to see it another, and so forth. But if you join all those elements together at the same time you have a completely different perspective.

Consider the Buddhist concept of 'concentration'. This isn't mental concentration in the normal sense; it's the gathering together of all the sense perceptors in one place within the body, which is that stillness and emptiness. It's like taking the colours of the spectrum, putting them on a disk and spinning them so that there is complete white. In the same way, here there is a massive clarity that enables us to see things that we couldn't otherwise know.

This is the grand awakening, when all these things come together. Then there is no separateness.

I am not asking you to believe this. I don't want you to believe. It's something for you to ponder. I don't want belief at all. If you ponder things and look for yourself you'll discover whether it's true or false. If it's false, that's fine – reject it and tell me I am wrong. I don't mind – I might be deluded (laughs).

It is not a vast change. You're already only a step away, and this is the next step. It is normal. When did the baby become the boy, the boy become the teenager, the teenager a man? It was normal in every way. Every day along the way your life has been ordinary, and yet you are totally different to what you were. In the same way, when you take the next step it will be ordinary, nothing spectacular. How could it not be? Unless of course there was a sudden transformation, which would probably drive you mad, since the difference would be so vast.

We've reached a point now where we are moving on to the next stage. This is why the world is in such a troubled state at the moment. It's preparing for the end of one phase and the beginning of a new, which will quietly overlap. Throughout the past, civilizations have died and new phases have begun. This is the point we are at now. I don't know precisely what is going to happen next but I am well aware that we're reaching the end of our civilization. But it doesn't mean to say the end of the world – nobody said that. The world is moving so fast now that it has to come to some sort of an end, and then start up again.

In the process, the human race will begin to change emotionally and mentally so as to be able to appreciate the spirit far more than the physical. That will become so much easier. We are certainly at a momentous point in history.

Seeing Clearly

I have been reading about Tantra recently. It's very inspirational to see yourself as a deity and to bring that divine nature into ordinary experience.

One sees these deities, as you might call them, and realises that one isn't other than them, but not them. Not so, but not other than so. This is a paradoxical way of being. But it has to be that way, on the simple basis that we're dealing with two different aspects – in Buddhist terms, the unborn and the born, the unmanifest and the manifest, the spirit and the physical. They are totally different dimensions and yet you have the two together.

Which one am I? Until this one is relinquished I won't be wholly that. Whilst this is contained within the physical, I can't claim to be wholly spirit. I'm both, depending on which side you look. On the one side it's heads, on the other side it's tails, but it's the same coin. It's not separate, just facing in different directions. We turn from one to the other, whichever face comes up most – if we have to deal with the world, we deal with the world. If we have to deal with spirit, we deal with spirit.

Of course, one sees things in a different way: most of the time one sees from the aspect of pure consciousness, seeing that which is apparent as being only apparent and not real. Like this table *(taps table)* – it's solid, but still apparent, because within it one sees something of the emptiness from which it arose. If you lived wholly in the physical realm, you wouldn't see that – you would see the table as merely solid. But when one looks at it from the point of view of consciousness, you see it as it is, empty. To a degree, all things contain that emptiness.

In the same way, you're sitting here this evening, and I'm sure there have been moments when you have felt as a whole – moments when you have been in unity and rapport with the feel of the place, when you have felt wholeness at the same time as perceiving separateness. Which one is real? In this state, you're not sure. In this dimension, it's neither this nor that – perhaps a bit of both, or maybe a little more of this than that *(laughs)*. But it's still very ordinary, on both sides. A bit of a joke, isn't it? *(Laughs.)*

But along the way, try to just examine things from an objective, observing point of view, without endeavouring to form opinions about them. Then you'll see the nature of this, this, this, this, and you'll see that it's not your normal ego-self that's looking, which would create a greater sense of separation rather than connection. As you become more still, with less thought, just observation, you begin to make progress. You begin to realise that the world is not quite the way you thought it was.

It's very limiting if you don't examine your life.

When you identify things, in a normal fashion, it is extremely limiting. And you don't realise the things you are missing. A wall you've seen every day of your life can look completely different if you take a closer look. You've just seen a blank wall, but now you see features and impressions you never knew were there. In the same way, if you look more closely at a person, you find they're not what they appear to be on the surface. Rather than dismissing them, you see that there is something deeper under there, something worthwhile. Look that little bit deeper and more carefully, rather than leaping to judgments. When you go beyond identification you find, "Hold on a minute, it's not quite that." You understand things a little better.

There are so many things we can deal with here: food, for

instance. If you're eating a meal quietly, focus your attention on exactly what you're doing: lifting food from the plate, putting it in your mouth, swallowing and chewing and so on. This will show you how taste is related to smell. Does smell come first, before the taste, or taste before? Does one influence the other? There are so many little things to be seen in the whole process.

There is so much to examine within your own experience, rather than just accepting it as it appears. It's very interesting, not just to look at these processes in their own right, but because this kind of examination sharpens your consciousness. You can use this sharpness in other areas, so that you can see all things in greater depth than normal. It needs practice, like everything else. In the same way that you have to build up your muscles to carry heavier weights, you need to practise with your consciousness to see things more deeply.

And this is the way that you do it: by looking at things that are already there, which you never really noticed, which you just accepted and took for granted.

Chapter 14

The Buddhist Society of Manchester

One evening I went over to John's flat – a basement flat in Brixton – and he told me, "There's somebody I'd like you to meet, a lady who's come down from Manchester, on her way to Bournemouth."

An hour or so later the lady came down. It was Connie Waterton. She was a founder member of the Buddhist Society of Manchester.

We talked for hours, comparing notes, and I found that there was another person who understood me, who knew exactly what I was talking about when I explained how I saw the world. Connie made me feel that there was a group in Manchester who would be very welcoming, who I could communicate with and feel at home with. So I decided to head up to Manchester, on New Year's Eve, 1957. Connie put me up, and after a few days I found a job at Kellogg's.

The Buddhist Society of Manchester began after the war, when food rationing was very tight and there was a series of lectures on diet. A group of people attended them and found there was a rapport between them, and decided to study other things together. They studied Buddhism with the help and guidance of a Burmese monk, U. Thittila, and inaugurated the society in 1951. One of the members took the robe in Thailand, Bhikkhu Kapilavaḍḍho, and started the English Sangha.

Connie was 16 years older than I, a very small woman, a Leo, with very piercing eyes. When she looked at people, they were initially afraid of her, because of her eyes. They thought she was looking through them, at their darkest secrets. But she was actually looking at the light within. She could see the very nature of what was happening. She had such a loving quality, the softest heart of anyone I've ever known, and an unbelievable intuitive understanding of other people.

Connie was very important in promoting Buddhism in the UK – she organised the first summer schools and the first intensive meditation retreats. She helped to organise the visits of Bhikkhus to this country – in fact, she arranged with British Rail for them to have free passage up to Manchester. She held the first proper meditation weekends – in a hotel in Buxton – and organised the Sangha funds which paid for a house in Hampstead for the first Bhikkhus.

The London society had a different approach, and they looked askance at what the Manchester Society was doing. They were more academic, more study-based, a little like the Theosophical Society. That came from Christmas Humphreys – he'd wanted to take over the Theosophical Society and they wouldn't let him, so he formed the Buddhist Society. I'd hesitate to say anything negative about Christmas Humphreys though – he introduced thousands of people to Buddhism through his books.

Years and years ago, two men who had been in Dartmoor Prison came to the Manchester Society. Christmas Humphreys was a judge, and he'd sent both these men down, to hard labour. They told us that, after their trial, he'd come down to their cells to talk to them for a couple of hours, and surprised them by being so caring. He'd left an impression on them, so when they got out of prison and came back home to Manchester, they came to us. We helped them out – we lent one of them money to buy a barrow to start selling fruit on the streets of Manchester. So Humphreys was a good man.

It was only once they saw the first summer school was successful that the London society sat up and took notice, and started to take up meditation themselves.

Once Evans-Wentz – the anthropologist and translator of Buddhist texts – came up to Manchester to give a talk. He'd given a talk in London, and started off with the same intellectual approach. After five minutes he stopped dead in his tracks, looked around and said, "I am not getting anywhere am I?" Then he began again, in a completely different way. Afterwards, he said to Connie, "It's a wonderful change, to speak from the heart rather than from the head!"

The Buddhist Society of Manchester met in Connie's house – in fact, it still meets there today. I did feel at home there straight away – the first time I'd felt at home since being a small child. I knew it was where I was supposed to be. Now I had a purpose – to be there for other people so that they could gain something from me. That was the path I was meant to be taking, the one I'd tried to find.

As soon as I arrived, the members of the society put me through a type of inquisition, or initiation – they asked me questions continually for three days. One of the members was Cyril Bartlett, an architect, a great intellect and a great heart. After three days, I remember him saying, "I don't know why you've come here. We can't teach you anything." I could give them confirmation of the ideas they were reading and discussing.

Soon after my arrival in Manchester I opened a book by an Indian teacher I'd never heard of, Ramana Maharshi. There was a picture at the front of the book, and I recognised him straight away – it was the man I'd seen that night when I was full of frustration in my room in Finsbury Park, when I'd cried out for help. I assumed that somehow he was looking after me.

When I read more about him I found he was a very remarkable man. I've always felt deeply connected to him. I feel that his nature is always with me, though not as a person. In the meetings at the society, there is often a powerful warm silence, and within that silence there is a tremendous influence. I've wondered many times if that's Ramana's influence coming through, as if his nature is acting through me. Not his personality, but his nature. I think that's where my emanation comes from. I can't claim any wisdom or kudos for myself – it's not me, I don't have the skill. If anything, I feel humbled and privileged to serve as a channel. Ramana is another doorway, a channel from some huge spiritual source, whose whole nature is to nurture, to grow, to become, coming to life rather than death, although not necessarily in a physical form. From time to time, his presence has been felt by others at the society too. In fact, only a few days ago, a woman said she'd had the image of a man in her mind, but didn't recognise it. From her description, it was clear it was Ramana.

I lived in the house for 18 years, until Connie died. We had a platonic relationship, a spiritual partnership. We worked together very comfortably for a long time. When newcomers arrived at the centre, we assessed their needs, and were able to decide between us what the best course of action for them was, what type of meditation they should practise, and so forth. In those days, we met every night, every day of the week, sometimes till the early hours of the morning. At weekends sometimes we went through the night without sleeping. It was a completely new role to me – a spiritual teacher, I suppose. I was allowed a free hand, and learned a lot as I went along. I picked up one or two modes of meditation, and invented some of my own.

There was no knowledge. My mind was still an empty bank. It's as though your mind is empty but clear and sharp and so able to notice phenomena you would never believe existed. They aren't so much things but qualities of a very subtle kind. Just as a person can instinctively sense certain factors about other people through their feelings, this doesn't operate through intellectual recognition but from the unconditioned realm. Consequently it doesn't carry any knowledge of things; but as soon as requested, it picks up vibrations, feelings, intuitions. I don't know exactly how it happens. It's not knowledge I've built up, but something which comes through me. I assume it is pure consciousness itself, speaking through this body, even to the point that – and this surprises more than anything else – from time to time I've found myself speaking particular words which I have no knowledge of, in the right context. And when I check, I find that it was the right usage.

I've also picked up on one or two episodes connected with Jesus Christ, quite different to the Bible, but hidden in the Jewish Torah. When I've spoken to people who've investigated, the information has been confirmed. Out of this, I began to see the true consciousness, and to understand that there is a record of all things which have ever been said or done. This record exists in the atmosphere, and is therefore available for all time to anybody who has the ability to touch into it. This is what is sometimes called the Akashic records. This is how one can remember previous lifetimes. Where does this memory live? It's not in this body, it's in the ether.

For the first few years in Manchester, I sat very quietly in the corner, listening to what was going on. If people asked me questions, I would respond, but most of the talking was done by others. But gradually I began to open up. Over the years, and as the original members faded away, the circumstances changed. It was no longer so traditionally Buddhist, and I began to come into my own. I didn't come through the traditions, but from a direct path. So I started to show people this direct method, so that they didn't have to go around the houses, through the traditions. As it has developed of itself, it's become quite unique, based on feeling rather than words. It involves appreciating people in the depth of their feelings rather than in their thoughts or understanding. I'm not interested in knowledge. It's not teaching, it's *showing* – introducing people to the deeper levels of their own being. I don't want people to learn anything, I want to open them up to see their own true nature. Patience has to come in – it can take years. You have to wait until the moment is right. Then I begin to reveal their nature more and more, until they realise that it's already there.

Gradually I persuaded the society members to ignore the books; for a long time I was completely opposed to books. I used to say, "Don't read anything, just look into your experience. Forget the theory, it just takes you further away." So the group became purely experiential.

I was eternally grateful to Connie. She taught me love, which mellowed me and gave me a deeper insight. Because of my difficult early life, I was inclined to be harsh. She also gave me a home. Before I came to Manchester, I had never been in one place for longer than two years. Coming here was like joining a family – and that's how it still feels now.

I was working during all these years, but the work was always secondary, just a means to an end. Most of my working life was spent with an engineering firm. At first they made joints for boilers, gaskets for valves, conveyor belts for coal mines and various other things. I started on the ground level, designing tools, making the materials by hand, but eventually I was managing the whole of the shop floor, doing all the stock keeping, directing the rest of the workers, as well as travelling around to paper mills, recovering large rollers on site. My colleagues didn't know anything about my other work as a teacher. They sensed I was different, but I don't think they could pinpoint how. They all accepted me, and I had a good relationship with them. They saw me as a sympathetic ear, someone they could come to with problems. It was as if they felt I would listen to them without any judgment. Sometimes I wouldn't even have to speak. They would talk through their issues and walk away, as if they'd realised a solution to the problem themselves. They seemed to benefit from the calmness of my presence and the full attention I gave.

I still do that now. Whenever I encounter someone, whether it's the girl on the till in the supermarket, the bus driver or a workman who comes to the house, I always give them my full attention, always look them in the eye and speak directly to them. It's amazing how they react – their faces light up, and they always send back benevolence to me.

After I'd been in Manchester for 18 years, Connie became seriously ill. She worked as the head librarian at the Teacher's College in Manchester. The managers decided the library needed painting, which had to be done during working hours. They installed some chemical dryers, which released a vapour. Connie developed a rash and was given some antihistamines. We didn't realise that one of their side effects was tunnel vision.

One day in the centre of Manchester, she was crossing the road and, because of her vision, she didn't see a tanker approaching. It hooked her up and threw her to the ground. I went to Salford Royal Hospital and found her on a trolley in a draughty corridor, one side of her black with bruising. She'd been there without water or using the toilet. I took her home and called a doctor. He was appalled and did the best he could. There were no bones broken, but within a few months she was very, very ill, and couldn't work. Before the year passed she was virtually bedridden. I looked after her – made her food, helped her eat, changed her clothes and her bed sheets, took her out in her wheelchair, almost everything. Then one day she fell in the bathroom and broke her bone just below the hip. An ambulance took her to hospital, where they did an X-ray and found that she was suffering from osteomyelitis, which was eating away at the bone itself, and the bone couldn't be joined again.

The interesting thing was, she refused all painkillers. She wasn't in pain. I overheard the nurse speaking to a doctor about it, wondering how on earth she could cope with the pain without medication. But Connie wasn't suffering.

She died two weeks later. I was by her side for the last two days, and with her at the moment she passed away. She was conscious right up to the last, her eyes completely bright. She quietly slipped away. I could tell by her eyes that she wouldn't be coming back again.

Those last two years of her life were very tiring, nursing her at the same time as keeping the society going and trying to earn money. I lost so much weight I was like a walking skeleton. Shortly after her death the solicitors arrived with her will. She had left the house to me.

Around that time, I heard that there was a Cambodian monk stuck at the university. This was Chandawana – "he of the face of the moon." It was the time of Pol Pot and the Killing Fields, and he'd been cut off from funds from home. Our government would do nothing to help him, so I took him into the house in Sale. I told him he could stay for as long as necessary, until he'd decided what to do. It made sense, because after Connie's death I was too exhausted to continue teaching so intensively. I was very impressed with Chandawana, and that seemed to be reciprocated. In fact, he paid me a great compliment. In a letter he sent from America years later he said he'd learned more about Buddhism from a year here than he did in all his life in Cambodia.

Around that time – in 1976 – I got married to Joyce. She was a member of the society, and during the months of Connie's illness she was invaluable with her help and support. I always knew she was a spiritually developed person. I moved into Joyce's house, and passed on Connie's house to the Buddhist Society of Manchester, which still owns it today.

A lot of people have mentioned that they sense Connie's presence in the house. It's not surprising – after all, she was born in the house, and spent her whole life there. And on top of that, she was a very spiritually developed person, one of the few who won't have to return.

Chapter 15

The Spiritual Universe

Possessions that Possess Us

I'm reading a book which says that spiritual awareness is slowly but surely spreading round the world.

It's true, in many different ways, if you can only recognise them. There is a basic instinctive movement taking place in people; it isn't being taught, it's coming out of them. It's a sense that "There must be something more", which of course there is. It's becoming lighter, and spreading throughout the world – even though, on the surface, things may seem to be getting worse.

As he presently is, man is not a creator, but a destroyer. He cannot accept things he does not want. He wants to destroy everything he does want. Looking at it Biblically, when the Israelites went into Palestine, they were told, "Here is the land in which you may dwell." They weren't told, "This is your land." But man likes to possess for himself, and to say, "This is mine."

In reality, there is nothing which is his; he comes in with nothing, he goes out with nothing. How can we possess anything? The North American Indians understood it better. They believed that the Great Spirit created everything. It all belongs to the Great Spirit. We can have the use of these things, but we do not own them. Therefore when we use them we must pay our compliments, and give our thanks for the blessing of the use thereof.

Whether primitive or highly evolved, we can still take that attitude. Why do we need to possess anything? All we need is a degree of comfort, to keep warm in winter, some food and drink to keep ourselves going, some company... None of these things have changed, although our methods of achieving them have altered. We have developed tools to make life easier, gadgets to save time, to give us more time for leisure, to communicate more quickly – although ultimately these tools have enslaved us. They're not servants anymore, and we can't be lazy anymore, so we become dissatisfied, working longer and harder than we ever did. Is this progress? We have to accumulate more and to earn more in order to safeguard what we have already accumulated. Again, do we possess things, or do things possess us?

God

Call it God if you wish; that's fine when you consider that, in the Hebrew sense, God means the indefinable, that which cannot be known or understood. The universal consciousness is not easy to understand, and yet we can know it. We can regard it as empty, in the way that the space in the room is emptiness. You're accustomed to emptiness, you know what it is. But *how* do you know? Do you think it's empty? You don't, because "empty" is only a word; it's meaningless. Is it possible that within the consciousness of the mind, it is empty of all ideas and concepts and knows the spacious element of emptiness as itself, so that the two are as one? When you actually experience emptiness, just for a moment, there is a sense of "Oh yes, I know." It does not need a word, does it?

We can refer to the Biblical words, "In the beginning there was a blankness on the face of the deep." A strange expression, meaning emptiness, or no-thing. Then comes the Word, a vibratory sound, and the word was God – *"was* God", not produced by God. So in the aspect of so-called creation, God appears before anything else, apparently, and then there is the whole process: let there be light, let there be this and so forth, for the so-called six days, before the seventh day of rest.

So this God created everything. But if there was nothing there, what did he create the world out of? Is it possible that there was only that conscious element of space that manifested itself, rather than creating something separate, so that now there is nothing manifest as physical, sentient or insentient, that isn't part of that one thing? A bit like couch grass – there might be one root a mile long with lots of tufts of grass and each tuft of grass appearing to be separate; but really it's all connected. Are we not all that one consciousness? Is it a possibility?

A few years ago I realised the true meaning of something I had been taught from the Bible when I was a little boy: the Biblical saying, "Not a bird falls from the bush that the Father is not aware of," the father being God or the Universal Spirit. If everything had been created, the bush, the bird, so many billions of different things, how could God possibly know them all, as separate creations? But if they were all manifestations of itself, it would be impossible *not* to know them.

If God created all things he could not know them, because they would be separate from him. Therefore he had to manifest himself as all things – as the tree, in which there was a branch, on which the bird sat, from which it fell. He was the bird, and the air through which it fell, and the ground. There was nothing but God, or consciousness. It is a manifestation of that being, but in a sense, the manifestation doesn't know. Only the consciousness knows.

So there was no creation, just a manifestation of that aspect of spirit. It makes no difference what form it takes, whether it is sentient or just a piece of rock; it is the spirit from which it came. So everything you touch is God, everything you see is God – God in terms of the unknowable, the conscious spirit, the great spirit, which is manifest in every way.

So there is nothing which is not a holiness. If we look at the world as a form of manifestation, does this contradict the Buddhist aspect of the unborn, uncreated, unmanifest? There is that which is born, which is created, which is manifest. There is a void; there is creation. It's the same. Or think in terms of atomic theory. At the atomic level, there is no such thing as a solid, just electrons and protons whirling around so fast they create the illusion of solidity. There are just whirls of energy in space. Is it so different after all?

So here we have science, the Bible and Buddhism – three different ways of seeing the same thing. Is it not possible that all things are as one?

Here and now, in this very room, every one of you is everyone else. You sense-feel the nature of what is here, do you not? How is this awareness possible if these bodies are separate? Alright, the manifest part is separate, because this body here is different from that.

We don't altogether live in oneness; we live in the thought area of separation, because thoughts are about things, not of things. But as we live, we feel. There is experience 'of things' and not 'about things'. So we experience or sense-feel that there is a living aspect of other beings – human beings, cats, dogs, even trees sometimes. There is a oneness, which we should try to live with more closely. Aren't we much more attuned to life itself rather than being at odds with it? This is what the Buddha taught, which is nothing to do with the belief system of Buddhism: to clarify the mind and see things as they truly are, so that we can sense, "Ah, this is not separate from me. I am."

Buddhism doesn't deal with spirituality at all; it deals with the hindrances that prevent you from gaining clarity of consciousness. Buddhism deals with the same Seven Deadly Sins as Christianity, but explains how to clear them away, to leave you with a clear consciousness. But the Buddha only went as far as the point of realisation of self-consciousness. Beyond that he never spoke, to my knowledge. The only indication that he was aware of other realms is where he was communicating with various spiritual entities. But that was personal, not connected to his teaching.

Buddhism will take you to an entrance point, after which you will begin to see the reality of the spirit worlds for yourself. There is nothing left other than that, because there is a realisation that your consciousness is spirit, wholly spirit, and is not separate from any other form of consciousness at all, but part and parcel. It is as if a raindrop falls into the ocean and becomes the whole ocean.

Chapter 16

The Next Step

I don't see myself as a Buddhist, although you could describe me as a follower of the Buddha. I appreciate wholly the Buddha's teaching. What I do find fault with is the orthodoxy of Buddhism, the dogma of the traditions. It's a little like Christianity and the Church. The Church doesn't understand the true essence of Christianity, and presents a false image of it. But anyone who follows the essential teachings of Buddhism and attains some clarity of consciousness will come to recognise the spiritual aspect of life and see it clearly for what it is. They will see themselves as spirit entities, not as physical ones. They will see that they are an integrated part of everything else, not separate.

A lot of people have gained merely by my presence. It's not really me as a separate entity which speaks. I don't have this knowledge, and by the same token I have no idea where it comes from. I know it is not mine, but I don't know of any particular being which imparts it through me. There have been occasions where I've been aware of entities around, but they have not entered into me. Sometimes entities of a very high order are present at our meetings, as many people will confirm. Entities don't speak through me, but I sometimes feel their influence, and translate it into words. I sometimes feel the influence of Ramana, but I don't feel that he is the source of the knowledge.

Knowledge is one of the most difficult aspects of this. We're so used to accumulating knowledge, to reading books and listening to teachers and collecting information – but I'm asking people to do the opposite. We're relinquishing knowledge, going into emptier and emptier spaces, creating areas of appreciation which cannot be known with any thought or understanding.

Consciousness exists in several different dimensions at once, one of which is the physical world. I live in these dimensions, not just in the physical plane. Consciousness is continually widening its expanse. One becomes more and more conscious, but not as an individual. Ultimately there is no self-consciousness, and no self. The only reality is consciousness itself, with no separation. When a person meditates deeply they lose awareness of the body and become part of this expanse of consciousness. They become aware that what they thought was their own consciousness is a part of Consciousness itself. It's in the ether; it comes in with the air you breathe. You can go without food for several months, without water for perhaps a month, but you can't go without air for a single minute – because the air is consciousness.

It's always assumed that thinking is consciousness but if this is true, how do you know when you're thinking thoughts you don't want to think? If you look at the nature of that which is looking, it is quite serene and unconcerned, looking at something which is chaotic. The two natures are different. Consciousness and thought are not the same. In a state of anxiety, consciousness contracts so much that it becomes nothing. In moments of peace and contentment, it expands so much that it becomes everything.

My mind is empty all the time. I think if I need to, otherwise I don't. I just enjoy the beauty of experience. When you think, your senses close down. If you think intently, you stop hearing, stop seeing. When you stop thinking, the world becomes intensely real and beautiful.

There may sometimes be difficulties, but there are no worries. Even difficulties are simple if you look at them clearly. Strangely, it appears that if one is able to clear the mind and have no knowledge whatsoever, the mind can respond immediately without thinking, and it is capable of doing that with no planning or forethought. In my experience, it always responds effectively and appropriately.

Silence is at the heart of everything. In mechanical terms, it's like a spinning wheel, as it moves up and down and around – there's the point in the middle which doesn't move.

There will be no next life for me. I don't want to come back; I want to go forward. That sounds suicidal in a sense, losing all aspects of a separate entity, to become a part of something far greater, but I'm quite prepared to let that happen. It's already happening, in fact. What you see as a separate person is already dissolving, like sugar into tea. So how could I come back?

The quality which was me will be available to all – not as an entity, but as a quality. I will still be there to help. It will come through other people, just as the influence of other people comes through me. Where else would it go?

In a sense I'm looking forward to it – not that I'm going to bring it forward. I've glimpsed the process between death and birth, even though I've never seen it wholly, just in the sense of reincarnation. I'm beginning to realise that this time around my being will quietly dissolve itself into the whole atmosphere.

What I'm doing here is helping a group of people to see in this fashion, to realise that there is something of a different nature beneath the surface, something unseen which is helping to prepare for the human race's next step in evolution. It's a matter of influence, helping to bring about a shift in human consciousness. It involves working with certain entities who shall remain nameless.

In the future people will become much more aware of the spiritual part of their nature. It could take a hundred years, possibly a few centuries, but eventually a shift will take place. I am convinced that it will only take a small number of enlightened people to shift the human race to a higher level – perhaps only 20 or 30 fully realised people. There will be many who go deeper down while others go upwards; those who go down will be lost; those who rise up will transform and flourish. It will happen – there's nothing to worry about.

But this is only a small part of what is going on. I'm not just working in the physical area, but in a dimension which has not yet come to be. But it will come to be. It will become manifest in the physical world. To some degree it's happening already, since here and there people are beginning to undergo this shift. They're looking beyond the teachings, looking for a way out. There's an urge inside them which is not yet fully manifest.

It may well be that before we reach this stage, an awful phenomenon will wreak havoc on the human race. But there has to be some sort of chaos before a shift occurs. There has to be a degree of death before rebirth. Death shouldn't be seen as final; it's part of a process of change. Its purpose is to bring about a great shift. Within everyone's body, their physical body, death is taking place every moment of the day. And this constant death allows regeneration. Every cell is completely changed – blood being the quickest, and the nails, hair, skin. So death is a part of the living condition; it's not a frightening phenomenon. Even thoughts – they arise, they come to be, and then they die again. The same with emotions. We have to face death before we have a renewal. Chaos isn't necessarily a state of despair, but one of hope.

This process will involve a shift in the human psyche, whereby people will much more readily see the spiritual nature within them, rather than being immersed in the physical. We will expand our consciousness so that we can see beyond the shadows, into the light.

It isn't just me. There are many people around the world working in the same way.

There are things which seem ordinary to me, but which appear extraordinary to others. In my presence, people become very attentive. I'm not entirely sure what they see or experience. They simply sit quietly, and seem to absorb an atmosphere like a gas. Everyone becomes immersed in it, and the room is filled with a powerful stillness and peace. It's as if I'm a catalyst. I become quiet, and the quietness spreads to everyone. Enlightenment is ordinary, even if it might seem extraordinary to the onlooker.

I'm 93 now, and it's more than 60 years since I underwent that shift. But it hasn't been static. Over the years, new things have emerged, and I've begun to see in greater depth. One begins to look into more profound areas, to reach realms which one never knew were there, or to see the same thing but with more clarity. There's always something beyond. I'm beginning to wonder if there will ever be an end.

When I look at my life, until the age of 29, there was utter desperation. There was some contentment in my early years, when we lived in poverty but had the richness of family life. I couldn't have wished for better parents, and it was a shame they couldn't stay around.

But since I underwent the shift, there has been peace. My purpose has been fulfilled – I am one with the nameless. I know the process I've been a part of won't be completed while I'm on this earth, but it's heading in the right direction, and I assume it will happen. My role in the process is almost finished. My influence will remain, as a wider consciousness which will enter into everybody, not as a personal consciousness. I won't be coming back, but I'll still be here.

Chapter 17

A Visitation

Real Mindfulness

Real mindfulness is to be aware of a situation both internally and externally, and so to see as a whole. That completeness is metta, loving-kindness. Metta is the wholeness of things, without separation. So there has to be the realisation of the wholeness of things, that *this* is not separate from *that*. You find that this wholeness is totally accepting, and in it there is the arising of wisdom.

When there is full mindfulness, there is nobody doing, no sense of self or ego. The self is not there – as a result, there is the complete union of everything, because everything is not seen and understood *out there*, but brought within and experienced as itself. This is true metta or love, and it is so balanced that it doesn't require anything to be done. That is the way it is. But of course it is only momentary. Once the mind latches on to this state, its nature changes and we return to duality. But in that moment there was union, and the feeling was different. When duality returns, the ego arises and it is uncomfortable. It has lost metta.

It is only when the mind accepts everything that it can become itself, and know its own nature. Everything is the mind's own nature, but with so many different facets. The mind visits here and it visits there, in and out of itself, and every so often it experiences co-joining. It's only when we have this expansion that we are aware of boundlessness. Only then is full consciousness present. But there is nobody doing it, is there? It just happens.

The real trick is to not come out of this state, to remain in it and see the whole world from its standpoint. One problem though is that you cannot pinpoint any single state for more than a moment because you have to see all the peripherals that go with it and the conditions that support it. However you look at it, the state is part of a whole and doesn't have an individual identity – and neither do you!

The Unconditioned

It is possible to experience the almost unconditioned dimensions even whilst living in the world we know, on the basis that we begin to sense-feel that we are not wholly *with* the physical world, almost as though we are alien in the world, and don't really belong there. There is a part of us in some other place we can't identify, that feels much more comfortable.

You can sense a security somewhere. In a very subtle way, you're drawn back into that, further away from the world we know. We become aware of it as we withdraw from the sense perceptors, from grasping, clinging or feeling aversion. We know that if we move back towards it we feel more comfortable, and if we go forwards to the other we feel more uncomfortable. It's the iceberg principle, you might say – instead of looking over the top, you are withdrawing into the huge mass underneath, which goes into different dimensions. The consciousness that is me, or you, is the small part of the iceberg over the top of the water. The bit you are not conscious of is the huge part underneath, which goes into other dimensions, or spheres if you would prefer to call them that.

This 'something' isn't there in this physical world of conditioning. It isn't part of the conditions within us that are involved with the physical: possession/non-possession, greed, hate, lust, and so on. As we begin to release our hold on the world and all its conditions, we become gradually more conscious of this other area, that huge area of consciousness of which we are normally totally unconscious.

This isn't easy to talk about, but as we withdraw into this other area, we feel a sense of moving closer to a homely position, away from discomfort. It is through this experience that we begin to appreciate that the longing we always felt was for this. The trouble is that we always try to satisfy this longing in other ways, grasping into the world. It isn't there in the world, of course – it is back in *here*, within consciousness itself. So instead of going outwards with the sense perceptors we have to go the other way, and become more conscious inwardly. Then we begin to sense a dimension that is other than this physical one. (In actual fact there is more than one dimension there, but we won't go into that now. One more is sufficient for the moment!)

But the key is to withdraw, and within this withdrawal we feel more ease and peacefulness. Sometimes in meditation people reach a quiet place in which nothing seems to be missing, but then they come out of the state, and feel that something's missing again. The moment you grasp at anything you lose peace. But when you let go you drift into peace.

That is why we meditate, so that we can learn, by concentrating mildly – very mildly – upon some particular object, to feel sensitively, not forcefully, and move into other dimensions. It's not a question of thinking or understanding, but feeling.

In a sense, it's a spatial dimension. If you regard space as empty, how do you conceive it? Can you think it? You can't – but you can know it. Your mind can take on that quality, and become it, if only fleetingly. It is a direct knowing, within a moment.

Letting Go

All that is required is the ability to let go of that which is unwanted, and to become the other. That is your permanent state. The one that grasps is the impermanent one, because it keeps changing. If there are apparent problems and difficulties on the outer level, just let go. If they hurt, why hang on to them? If you grab a handful of nettles and they sting you, do you want to do it again? Let it go, let it go. It's not a question of throwing it away – just let go and it will drop out of the mind's grasp. And then you will develop a different attitude right away.

It's not easy though is it? The tendency is to think, "Oh, I must do that, just in case." The tendency is to try to put things right. But there is nothing to put right. It's just letting go of what's wrong. There was never anything to put right. It's removing the part that is covering the rightness up. That is the joke: it was always there. You don't produce it; it's just waiting to be uncovered.

The one thing it has is immense patience. You can go through millions of lifetimes, and it will still be there. The trouble comes from identifying with a physical body which is conditioned. The body will always be conditioned until it dissipates. But the consciousness doesn't have to remain with it. It can be out and about as well as within.

One problem I have is that I sometimes let myself get caught up in ambitions, goals for the future. I am aware that as soon as I get into that mode it creates unhappiness.

It does – it creates chaos. You think to yourself, "How should I go about this? Do I do this, that, or do something else?" Then you have a series of confusions. Learn to be content with where you are at the moment and there are no problems. That is the condition of desire, to want more. If you realise you have enough then you don't want more. The whole secret lies in that; letting go. Let go, let go. You can pick it up and take a look, then put it back again where you found it. You don't have to pick it up and put it in your pocket. Otherwise pretty soon you'll have full pockets.

You can know where the peace is, but you may not always be able to get there.

When you establish yourself in that peace you don't need any knowledge, because you can approach things with an open mind, an empty one, and see things as they truly are, without equating them with some past experience which doesn't apply today. You can deal with things as they ought to be dealt with, if they need dealing with at all. So there is no problem. There's just peacefulness, an empty mind. But in that empty mind whatever is there is experienced as being the experience of the moment, which is living your life. If you are thinking, you are not living your life at all; you're in a different world altogether. There is so much in this world that is very pleasurable just through the experience of it, just so long as you don't try to possess it, or are not averse to it *(laughs)*.

The peace has always been there, under the chaos. In a sense it's like the deep ocean: at the top there is turbulence, but down below it's serene. We are the same, precisely the same. We can live in a state of unbelievable serenity, which doesn't get disturbed in any way even if there is chaos all around us.

The Stillness

Here is a question for you: What happens when the 'I', your ego-self, meets the stillness? Where does the I go?

You can't find it, can you? If the two come together the ego dissolves. Then a different dimension emerges. If you can remain there, and deal with things externally, you deal with them in a totally different way, because you don't see them as separate. If you let go of the conditions, ego disappears entirely, if only momentarily. You lose the conditions that produce ego. In other words, you let go of them. The mind relaxes, disappears and, as it does so, it drops into peace.

All you need to do is observe the processes. Over time, that will bring you closer and closer.

I feel a great deal of satisfaction knowing I am on the right track.

That is to be expected, because you know that from the inside, not the outside. Your experience up to the present has proven that point. This means that you don't have to seek any more. You just have to live on and wait for it to show itself to you. Don't seek. Be open and allow things to be revealed to you. When you seek something, you have a vague idea of what you're looking for, but this is beyond anything you could imagine. It's beyond imagination. So be open about it and let it show itself to you! *(Laughs.)*

I feel that now I know the area where the wholeness lies. For many years it was a mystery.

That's fine. As you begin to see more and more of these things, then you feel a great deal more confidence. You are learning to learn. And of course we get a great deal of laughter out of it, which keeps us buoyant, not too serious.

There is Only Consciousness

This is only a recognition of the very fact, the very basic fact, that there is only consciousness. It's not that I am conscious; consciousness is what I am.

Can you put your finger on what consciousness is? You can't, can you? Let's say it's life – that's true, that is one aspect of it. Is there any life without consciousness? Or is there any consciousness without life? Or how about nothingness, or emptiness? It is still consciousness, but is there life in emptiness? Yes, there is, because consciousness gives it an energy that otherwise would not be there, though it is always as one *(laughs)*.

I was meditating yesterday, and just for a second I felt that my consciousness wasn't in my mind anymore. There was nothing in my mind. I felt I was part of something bigger.

Did it have a size?

No, it was everywhere.

That's right. If you experience for a moment this *everywhere* – being in the 'big everywhere' – is there any self?

No.

There wasn't anybody there, but there was consciousness. How could you experience it if it were not consciousness? The consciousness is not you. This is how we come by that strange saying, "Not I, but not other than I." It is true, isn't it? It is not really you, but it is being experienced through you.

It didn't feel spectacular or glorious.

No it's not. It is perfectly ordinary and everyday. It is always there and you know it was always there, because of these experiences. That is the whole point. That's good. With a bit of luck you might see more yet. I won't suggest anything. Do you feel comfortable in this expansive-ness?

Yes. It felt completely natural. It was like slipping out of a daydream into reality.

Exactly, that's what you are doing, but it takes a little while to appreciate. It takes a while for the old brain-box to become quiet *(laughs)*, and then it all comes flooding back. If you keep returning to that place, you'll eventually reach a point where you can turn it on and off at will. If you feel troubled, you can step out of the turmoil and enter into the peace. Very useful indeed. It doesn't interfere with life but it does tend to round off the sharp edges and make it more comfortable *(laughs)*.

The Visitation

These are interesting times, very interesting... Is anybody experiencing anything at the moment?

There is a strong flow through.

I'd like you to be a little more aware of what you are experiencing now. At the present moment, here in this room, there is quite a lot to be experienced. We are very fortunate tonight.

I felt something earlier, but I can't describe it.

Yes, it's not easy to describe, I appreciate. Just feel at ease. Just become aware that there is a presence available. Don't strain yourself, just relax, and quietly sense whatever there is...

(Several minutes of meditative silence follow.)

Now where did everybody go to?

I can't quite explain, but there was a unity, and a sense that each person had a counterpart... Is that the subtle body, or is it something else?

There was a kind of astral body around. You are perfectly

right.

I felt, and still feel, that the room is very full.

Yes, it is extremely full, and has been most of the evening. This is what I was waiting for people to sense. You can't put your finger on exactly what or who it is, but you know it is full. That's right.

I feel a tingling sensation.

It's not a normal sensation is it? It's almost as though it is not there, within the physical body. There is a sort of reverberation running through it, that's right. We are certainly moving into different areas now.

I felt that a way opened up. There seemed to be a lot of beings around, and I had the distinct impression that they were lining a way. Then, strangely, I saw a man of pure light walking up that way.

Good.

I felt a strong light inside me, that wasn't just inside. It was golden, shimmering, and it filled me with energy, with a strong feeling of well-being and radiant energy... Is it me or has the room suddenly gone cool?

Yes, entities are passing around. It's almost like a breeze on us, a cool breeze. This is the sensitivity I am looking for. These experiences are not imaginary; they are real. We've had a room full of entities this evening and they are moving around. Every now and then you can feel them, making themselves known. Once you experience these phenomena, you begin to appreciate the other realms, without bodies. Occasionally they may be seen as light but not as shaped, in the manner we would expect.

We've had a visitation of quite a few entities of the celestial order. They are beginning to leave now. I wanted to see if anybody was sharp enough to appreciate them, which indicates of course the degree of consciousness developing. Here and there, people will reveal some characteristics of the level they are at. It's surprising – each individual will be visited in a different way according to their level, and who and what they are.

So, a good evening as far as I am concerned! Things seem to be working. To quote from the Christian perspective: "Where a few of you are gathered together in my name I will be present." This is the presence of the spirit coming down in the form of entities of the celestial area, to assist us. When a group comes together and creates a rapport, this opens the door for these happenings, because we are open to receive. We're not pushing, which would close us off. When we are open to receive, the entities can descend. And a great deal of help can come this way. It helps us to move up to the next stage.

These entities are always willing to help people who are ready to be helped. They have never been born into the conditions we experience, but they have a readiness to come down and help those who are endeavouring to escape from these conditions. That seems to be their role. I'm talking casually, but there is a reverence and a love underlying my casualness. I feel the utmost respect for such entities.

These entities are of a much higher area of consciousness, and of course of intelligence. That is where intelligence lives – out there, not here. We only use it from time to time when it comes through. Intelligence is not an aspect of the conditioned world. It would not be conditioned if it were.

With human beings I am always conscious of negativity, but at this level there is absolute positivity. There is also a sense of great familiarity.

Yes. If there wasn't a difference you wouldn't be able to sense what was there. Can you imagine the negative being drawn into the positive, literally drawn in? A bit like a magnetic field, with one side seeking the other? That is what eventually will happen – all negativity will be drawn into the positive.

You see we have gone past Buddhism *(general laughter)*. The Buddha never spoke of things like this. He knew, but at that time it was not appropriate to speak of these things. Now certain people have become a little more developed, and are able to appreciate these phenomena.

All of this leaves a question, doesn't it? *Am* I really part of that, or a part of this, or both?

You will find out in due course. And it won't be a complete surprise either. It's nothing to be scared of – in fact, quite the opposite. This is one of the funny things about all this. Everybody has expectations of something absolutely marvellous, something explosive and beautiful. But in reality it's downright ordinary, everyday. The ordinary world is just seen in a different way, as homely rather than hostile. This ordinariness makes the state easier to attain, and more stable. Otherwise it would just explode and quickly disappear. A quiet realisation is far better than an explosive sense of wonder. An acceptance that this is the Real.

The End

My old friend, Father Time, keeps tapping me on the shoulder saying, "It's near your time." *(Laughs.)* "But I can't go yet – I still have things to do," I tell him *(laughs)*. Then he goes away again. I have to admit there is a tendency to be drawn into a different sphere altogether. But it's not time yet. I had the opportunity of going out, but decided to stay and finish the job and I'm going to stay until it is finished. I am getting near the end of it though, I must admit. A couple more years or so? We shall see. I'm wondering when it will just close down and then be no more. I suppose that is what will happen eventually *(laughs)*. It seems that the winding down process is beginning, put it that way.

I think there is a broad swathe following behind you.

In due course, we will all follow one another. Somebody has to go first to prepare the furniture, as you might say *(laughs)*. I have had a purpose for a long time, and I feel I have achieved most of it. It's not completed yet, I grant you. But it is very close to it, and once it is complete, I can't see any point in staying. I am not that important anymore. There are others here who can do just as well as I, though they don't know it yet.

Acknowledgements

I am very grateful to Dave Johnson of the Buddhist Society of Manchester, who recorded and then typed up many of the transcripts of Russel's meetings. Thanks also to Roger Barnes, Josephine Connolly and Susan Cain for their help with proof-reading. Most of all, thanks to Russel Williams for many years of guidance and inspiration, and for the opportunity to share his teachings in the form of this book.

Steve Taylor

BOOKS

O is a symbol of the world, of oneness and unity; this eye represents knowledge and insight. We publish titles on general spirituality and living a spiritual life. We aim to inform and help you on your own journey in this life.

Visit our website: http://www.o-books.com

Find us on Facebook:
https://www.facebook.com/OBooks

Follow us on Twitter: @obooks